DATE DUE			
MAY 1 0 1982			

Deafness and Learning

A Psychosocial Approach

Hans G. Furth

Center for Research in Thinking
and Language

The Catholic University of America

Wadsworth Publishing Company, Inc.
Belmont, California

Wadsworth Series in Special Education

Series Editor: Eli M. Bower
University of California, Berkeley

Published

Deafness and Learning
Hans G. Furth
The Catholic University of America

Forthcoming

Emotional Disturbance and Learning
Eli M. Bower

Designer: Gary A. Head

Editor: Sandra Craig

Technical llustrator: John Foster

ISBN 0–534–00231–5

L. C. Cat. Card No. 72–92680

Printed in the United States of America

2 3 4 5 6 7 8 9 10   76 75 74

Foreword

The heart hath treble wrong
When it is barr'd the aidance of the tongue.

Shakespeare, *Venus and Adonis*

Present concepts and confusions about handicapped children are the product of a rapidly retreating past and a surging future. Many of our notions about handicapped children were born and nurtured in times different from ours. Undoubtedly they were relevant and responsive to the presses and problems of that day. But the actions and reactions of today bring new choices and different challenges. If the world has changed radically for the majorities, it has changed more so for the minorities.

It is fatuous to look back into history with anger or derision. I'm old enough to remember our struggles three decades ago to establish and develop educational programs for the educable mentally retarded, the trainable mentally retarded, and the emotionally disturbed. Those battles were fought on different conceptual fields from those of today. Labels for fiscal or classification purposes are no longer as necessary; categorization for educational purposes are challenged and many hoary and beloved programs are dissolving into fresh but untried practices. The conceptual and educational meaning of "retarded intellectual development" is being reconsidered in light of research on language development, affective development, motivation, and self concept. Similarly, new research on the blind and the deaf and other handicapped children has produced a ferment and movement in the entire field.

Part of this energy and interest has been transmitted to undergraduate students and prospective teachers, physicians, and psychologists. In a sense this volume and those that follow were energized by students dissatisfied with available written materials on handicapped children. Traditional textbooks have almost always followed a pattern of presenting in a solid but stodgy descriptive fashion the concepts, etiologies, incidence, programs, social and medical definitions, and comprehensive arrays of research data. All of this is well done and useful but rarely does the material become intellectually stimulating and personally integrative to bright and committed students.

Our changing society moves faster for those with greater adaptive problems. Children with sensory, motor, or mental handicaps have more need for bold conceptual inventions and programs than others. Our goal in this volume and the others is to challenge our bravest and best minds to ponder and produce the concepts, the research, the educational and social changes that will benefit handicapped children.

This volume by Hans Furth is outstanding and dramatic. For a man who subscribes to thinking without language, Furth does quite well with it. He writes from inside the deaf person looking out at the noisy world and from the hearing person listening to the silence of the deaf. His is an artful, impassioned, and professional work. We are indeed fortunate to launch the series with this stimulating volume.

Eli M. Bower
Berkeley, California

Preface

One cannot write an "objective" book on a topic about which specialists have basic, far-reaching disagreements. This is even less possible when the subject matter is not merely a theoretical question, as, for instance, the relation of hearing loss to personality, but a question of practical application of psychological principles in education and preparation for life. In such instances the traditional, familiar ways are apt to be called objective and are not required to pass the scrutiny of critical justification, whereas novel approaches are often automatically viewed as one-sided or not scientifically validated.

I accepted the invitation to write a book on deafness for this series on special education because I wanted to treat the topic in a different way from the usual educational presentation. In fact, other books frequently start where this one leaves off. This book attempts to provide a solid theoretical foundation from which a more technical treatment of education can follow. Not all statements in the book are scientific in. a narrow sense. The first five chapters are designed to introduce the reader to the life and world of deafness in the United States. These chapters were written from a personal perspective based on observations of and research about deaf people for the past fifteen years.[1] To require scientific validity in this introduction would turn it into an unwieldly mass of statistical details, which in themselves are meaningless and, as everybody knows, are open to diverse interpretations.

I believe that a perspective that questions previously held assumptions is as scientific, often more so, than the opposite view. One can start by considering verbal language a necessary ingredient to a human life, and then one can look for deficiencies in intellect and personality as evidence

[1] It gives me pleasure to acknowledge the research and training support received over many years from the Social and Rehabilitation Services, U.S. Department of Health, Education, and Welfare. This agency deserves credit for taking initiative in launching research and training projects for deaf people.

for one's view. I would claim that this language hypothesis is a more "biased" view than a null hypothesis that starts with no assumption about the role of language and allows the observation of facts in a nonevaluative manner.

Take, for example, the fact that most deaf people in the United States typically find their spouses, friends, recreation, and social life among other deaf persons. In other words, they do not freely mix with the hearing world. Should one automatically judge this state of affairs as an indicator of personal and social maladjustment? It seems more scientific—not to say fair— to examine the deaf community on its own merits without preconceived theoretical notions. Observations of deaf persons may show that these notions are themselves mistaken.

In any case, the reader should have no difficulty separating research data and research interpretation from general observations and personal speculations. In fact, one purpose of the book is to invite the reader to come to grips with the assumptions and opinions surrounding the education of the deaf child. Whether the reader is a student of special education, a parent of a deaf child, or simply a person who is interested in the life of deaf people, I trust that this book will contribute to a better understanding of deaf children and adults. Only on this basis of a better psychological comprehension can we take constructive steps toward providing an appropriate educational and vocational setting for the deaf learner.

Hans G. Furth

Contents

Contents

7. Research in Personality and Social Aspects 72

Stereotypic thinking. Tact. Impulsivity. Verbal knowledge and emotional maturity. Mental health. Surveys of deaf people in various cities. Sources of ego strength. Socialization. Dimensions of personal interactions.

8. The Testing of Deaf Children 86

Standardization and use of tests. Intelligence tests. Scholastic achievement tests. Educational methods testing.

9. The Order of Priorities 101

In the parental home: acceptance of communication. In society: acceptance of deaf community. In school: acceptance of the thinking and feeling self. New educational goals.

Appendix 1: A Thinking Laboratory for Deaf Children 105

Appendix 2: Overview of Educational Opportunities for the Profoundly Deaf Child in the United States, by Sydney Wolff 113

Appendix 3: Behavior Inventory 120

References 124

Index 126

1

An Extraordinary Ordinary Family

Have you ever wondered how people in different societies and cultures live? Wouldn't it be fascinating to visit remote places on the globe to observe unfamiliar customs and strange tongues? We could learn much from such occasions, provided we were curious and tolerant. We could discover that many things we take for granted or consider necessary in our culture are by no means as universal as we had thought. We could learn to appreciate things that we had hardly perceived as worthy of our attention. Most important, we could experience that all human life is colored by the perspective peculiar to a person's own society. The educated person does not try to do away with this cultural-personal perspective—an impossible task—but he recognizes and analyzes it in himself and in others.

This is not easy. Children accept their way of life as normal and natural, and as adults they view events from within the framework of their perspective. Behavior or ideas that do not fit into this framework are considered strange or abnormal, or they simply remain unnoticed. A view that considered the earth as the center of the physical universe precluded the observation of many events of which a six-year-old child is capable today. In addition to this intellectual barrier, people have a strong emotional dislike of "strange" things. Thus it is not surprising that substantial intellectual or moral progress during human history invariably implied the overcoming of some traditionally ingrained viewpoint—a sort of intellectual or emotional revolution—which made it possible to see and accept new ideas.

The discussion so far applies to any person who is different or "strange" because of some physical disability. In fact, it is recognized by trained observers that society's reaction to the physically different person is a major factor, frequently *the* major factor, in the person's rehabilitation or failure to be rehabilitated. The discussion applies with particular validity to the deaf person. Of all physical disabilities, deafness is the only one that makes its members part of a natural community. Therefore, although we do not find blind or crippled subgroups in society, we are justified in referring to a deaf community as a societal subgroup. This major difference between deafness and other disabilities must never be forgotten. In the United States deaf persons are perhaps better organized than in other parts of the world, but regardless of country, deafness creates an underlying communality that provides for all but a few individuals a social-psychological basis of belonging. This belonging to a community is probably the single most important factor working in favor of the deaf individual. It is therefore a natural place to start our considerations of deafness.

Quite probably, unknown to you, deaf people live within a few miles of your home. Let us look at their life, particularly at their activities and communications at home and during leisure times. Such a visit can be as intellectually and emotionally rewarding as any trip to a foreign country. The first striking difference is of course the elaborate use of gestures. Contrary to what you may have thought, the typical deaf person communicates primarily by means of visible movements of the hands, fingers, face, and whole body. Here is a young deaf mother in lively conversation with a visiting deaf friend. They are reminiscing about the residential school they both attended—about mutual friends, impressions of teachers and other adults, interesting excursions, and activities of various kinds. At times, in the heat of conversation, both women talk and listen at the same time. Among deaf persons such simultaneous activities are easier and create less interruption than with us, because talking is done by gestures and listening by sight.

The conversation is taking place in the kitchen-dining area while the mother prepares dinner. The three-year-old son plays in an adjacent room, and mother keeps an eye on him. The little boy catches his mother's eye and exclaims, "I am starving." He accompanies his speech by moving his right hand down his chest toward his stomach. You observe the child's normal and clear articulation and rightly infer that he is not deaf. He is using signs all the same to make himself understood by his deaf parent. The mother replies by gesturing and making a sound which you can guess is meant to stand for "Just wait a little."

Shortly afterwards a bell rings, whereupon the boy excitedly cries out, "Daddy, daddy," and points to a flashing light connected to the bell. The mother notices the light and presses the button that opens the door downstairs. In a few moments the father enters the apartment and expresses delight at seeing an old school friend. He picks up his son, settles down in a chair with the boy on his lap, and joins the conversation with eagerness and interest. On his part, he reports some less happy news about the car accident of a mutual acquaintance, told to him by a deaf fellow worker at the plant. Every now and then the little boy partici-pates, but mostly he nudges his mother toward the stove.

As they finally sit down to dinner—three deaf adults who went to school together, two of whom married each other and have a hearing son—let us pause for a minute. After the first impression of strangeness due to the unfamiliar medium of communication, the observer notices an equally curious reaction of familiarity. You say to yourself, How can these people live without a verbal language and yet be so like us? For surely what took place during the late afternoon in the apartment of the young deaf couple could as easily happen anywhere across the country. You hesitate to identify your reactions precisely. Perhaps you expected deaf people to have overcome their handicap through schooling. You know that the primary aim of deaf education is the teaching of language, including speech and speech reading. But here you meet educated deaf adults whose speech and ability to read lips is apparently quite poor, so that oral communication between them and yourself would be difficult, if not actually impossible. If I tell you now that only a very small per-centage of deaf people comprehend the English language well enough to read, say, this book, you realize that our three deaf friends probably have a very inadequate knowledge of English. This arouses a second reaction, which lay dormant in the back of your mind and which was reinforced by your observation of the gestures: apparently then these deaf people do not know language and cannot speak. They are dumb. DUMB.

You think of the archaic phrase *deaf and dumb*. What does dumb mean? It means *mute*, a person who cannot speak. But traditionally we associate dullness of mind and stupidity with dumbness. A person without speech is like a dumb animal. Well, wait a minute. If we find ourselves in a strange country, is not our speech useless and do we not consequently become dumb? Not quite, for we do have speech, or better, language, and thus even though we cannot use it for communication, we can use it for private purposes. Perhaps then deaf persons differ from hearing per-sons primarily in that they employ a different language. But do our deaf friends have a language? Their knowledge of English is woefully poor, and gestures alone can hardly be called a language—at least, it must be a primitive language compared to society's verbal language. Hence, this second reaction gives you a chilly feeling of strangeness that does not fit into your familiar perspective: "Man is the speaking animal; lan-guage differentiates man from beast." A deaf person who does not know a verbal language and who uses primarily a primitive concrete gesturing is perhaps only half human.

But then again, our deaf people behaved so normally. How could they do it without the education that verbal language assures? I want to leave you with this third reaction, the puzzlement that a severe lack of language does not automatically cause a severe lack of traditionally expected conduct. We shall come back to these three types of reactions and work them through very carefully, because your whole attitude toward deafness is colored by them. The primary aim of this book is to make you aware of these reactions and to help you discover the underlying reasons and assumptions.

In the meantime dinner is over. Mother puts the child to bed after playing with him for a little while. Attached to the bed is a microphone that transmits sound above a certain level of loudness to a light signal in the living room, to which the two other adults have retired. In this manner the deaf parents can "hear" distress signals from their child and can keep in touch with him. Modern technology makes the life of deaf persons easier. You think of hearing aids. Only the man wore an aid, and he removed it as soon as he was at home and does not put it on later when he goes out again. Your guess that hearing aids cannot be a simple answer to the problem of hearing loss is reasonable. The man wears the aid chiefly to become aware of sudden noises at work, whereas the two others have found that hearing aids are of no functional benefit and they never wear them. The man leaves now to attend a meeting of the Deaf Athletic Club, of which he is an active member, both as organizer and as tennis player. As he gets into the car and drives to the clubhouse you may wonder that a deaf person is allowed to drive at all.

Again, this is a normal reaction. A deaf person would not hear the sound of a horn in another car or even the warning signal of a fire truck or a police car. For these and similar reasons deafness used to be a legal obstacle to getting a driving license in many states and countries, although today a deaf person can obtain a license in all the United States and Canada. However, insurance is a major problem, as it is for many physical disabilities. The deaf community in the U. S. has solved this problem in typical fashion, first by creating their own association for purposes of life insurance and then by lobbying as an association for their legal rights. What about their driving record? Does not a lack of hearing contribute to a greater accident rate? The facts show that deaf drivers have a better record than others. The small disadvantage of not hearing is apparently more than compensated for by greater visual vigilance. Consider for a moment: if you could not hear the siren, you would still notice the peculiar reaction of the other cars and would behave accordingly.

Nevertheless, the world being what it is, if a deaf driver is involved in an accident the first reaction is, "Why does the state allow a non-hearing person to drive? Lack of hearing must have been a contributing cause to the accident." One need not be a genius of a lawyer to present this specious reasoning as plausible to a jury of hearing persons who need not be any more prejudiced than you or I. When one sets out to put the blame on another, a physical defect is a natural target. This then is another reason why deaf people are doubly careful and alert to avoid accidents: they know that in spite of favorable statistics, the law and the insurance companies look at the deaf driver if not with bias at the least with an unfriendly eye.

Our deaf tennis player has arrived at the clubhouse, where some members who have already gathered welcome his arrival. In a few minutes they sit down at a large table and discuss club business in formal parliamentary procedure. This is indeed a fascinating sight—a room filled with close to twenty persons, all engaged in a lively discussion, or rather a series of frequently simultaneous discussions, by means of gestures and signs and hardly a sound. The main item on the agenda is the Deaf Olympics to be held in Scandinavia the next year. The members note your presence, and you are introduced to the chairman as a visitor. They nod and smile at you and seem rather pleased at your interest in the deaf community. They even try to gesture to you and engage you in conversation.

You notice that the chairman articulates rather well, and you infer correctly that he lost his hearing after the onset of speech. This "adventitiously" deaf person acquired speech and language as you and I did, although later, while he was still young, he lost his hearing. He is now a member of the deaf community, but he differs from the "born" deaf in that he feels at home in a verbal language in a way that is quite rare for others. For this reason he often assumes the role of community leader within deaf organizations. There seems to be no end of such organizations for and of deaf persons—local, national, international. This spirit of cohesiveness makes sense because of the difficulty of communication in the verbal medium as compared with the apparent ease of communicating in the gestural medium.

As you leave our deaf friends you come away with positive feelings about deaf people in the U. S. There is no reason for pity or rancor. You may find it difficult to imagine how a child can develop without the language of society, but now that you have glimpsed the life of deaf adults you no longer doubt that deafness is a condition that a person can successfully accept and accommodate to. And if by chance—perhaps for personal reasons—you find yourself making what is really a senseless comparison—Is it worse to be blind, or deaf, or to have cerebral palsy, or whatnot?—you can at least point to some constructive things that are a direct result of early deafness.

Deaf people themselves have always felt this way. They cherish a spirit of pride and independence. They are the only group I know of that lobbied against receiving tax benefits. When there was a movement afoot to give to deaf people a tax bonus similar to the one that legally blind persons receive, the associations of deaf persons persuaded the legislators to drop the matter. "We do not want any special privileges," they implied. "We want to be treated as fairly as other persons in the land."

It would be foolish to deny that early profound deafness is a serious disability that puts many burdens on the deaf child and his parents. We shall mention some of the obstacles to be overcome in subsequent chapters when we trace the development of a deaf child as he grows up in this country.

2

Words and Concepts in Deafness

Precise terminology is a necessary prerequisite to the understanding and accurate communication of a topic. If appropriate words are lacking, we are able to analyze the underlying thinking and produce new words. The field of special education—including the sphere of language and hearing impairment—abounds with words that can be assigned a wide range of meanings, so that we must explain the particular sense in which we use these words.

Deafness refers to a functional hearing loss of sufficient severity to prevent aural comprehension of speech even with hearing aids. When this degree of deafness is present at birth or very early in infancy it effectively precludes the spontaneous acquisition of verbal language through the normal channel of hearing. *Early profound deafness* or *prelingual deafness* are reasonable terms to describe the bulk of today's population in schools for the deaf and in the deaf community at large.

This was not always the case. A hundred years ago the majority of deaf persons became deaf in childhood through illnesses that are now better controlled, which meant that these adventitiously deaf persons had acquired language before the onset of deafness. If a person knows a language, it is practically impossible for him to forget it or not to use it, although his speech may deteriorate and may become nearly incomprehensible. For these persons speech in its expressive and receptive phases is the main problem. However, for children who have early profound deafness language, not speech, is the difficulty. You can simulate how it feels to be an adventitiously deaf person by watching television with the sound turned off; your problem is to read lips. But if you want to simulate how it feels to be a prelingual deaf person you must watch the screen of a foreign television station. Your problem now is not merely to read lips; even if you could, you would still be faced with the task of comprehending the language.

Of course hearing impairment is only rarely an all-or-none affair.

The hearing mechanism is extremely complex and is only imperfectly understood. Audiologists measure hearing loss in *decibels,* a scale of intensity of loudness. They measure the loss for each ear, for different frequencies (pitch), and by different methods. An audiogram provides a graphic display of the results of testing, and in some cases the physiological locus of deafness can be inferred from characteristics of the audiogram.

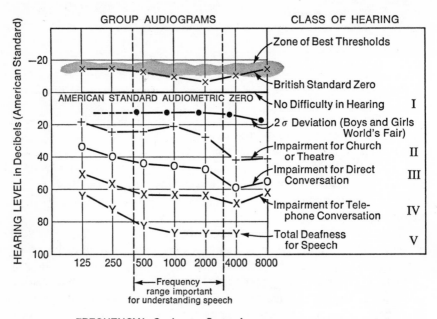

Figure 2.1.   Self-classification of Hearing Impairment. These group audiograms show the average hearing levels of the subjects in the United States Public Health Survey (*Beasley, 1936*), who classified their own hearing according to Captions I to V at the right. From H. Davis and S. R. Silverman, *Hearing and Deafness* (New York: Holt, Rinehart and Winston, 1960), p. 254.

To summarize the test results the audiologist refers to an average hearing loss across the frequencies of speech. To give you a rough idea (putting aside for the moment a million distinctions and subjective conditions), we would consider a person with an average hearing loss of 80 or more decibels in the better ear as profoundly deaf; a hearing loss of around 60 decibels would be called a case of severe hard-of-hearing or moderate deafness; a hearing loss of around 40 decibels would indicate a moderate hard-of-hearing case and of around 20 decibels a case of light hard-of-hearing.

These numbers are merely tentative indicators of hearing status, but they illustrate that ranges overlap within a continuum that stretches from a residual hearing of zero, or total deafness, to profound and moderate deafness, and to the twilight zone of hard-of-hearing status. The accompanying figure illustrates the use of the decibel scale in relation to hearing impairment. What additional considerations contribute to proper diagnosis of hearing status? We can distinguish among (1) the mere hearing of a certain intensity of sound, (2) the discrimination of a particular sound, especially a speech sound, and (3) the understanding of the spoken message. Speech is a complex sound pattern that occurs in rapid, sequential order and involves what we can call the transformation of perceived sound into the hearing of meaningful speech. This process not only implies a knowledge of language that can be considered as separate from hearing but is itself a vital aspect of hearing, without which functional hearing of speech is impossible.

Turning from physiological to subjective factors, there is the first age, or onset, of hearing loss, an important divide in terms of language acquisition. Postlingual hearing loss does not substantially affect a person's knowledge of his first language, whereas prelingual severe hearing loss makes the acquisition of this knowledge a severe problem. Another factor is the use of residual hearing, with or without hearing aid. Elements such as the type of training and when it begins, individual differences in abilities and personality traits must also be considered.

When the hearing system functions perfectly, the acquisition of language is so normal and spontaneous that individual variations in aptitudes or personality do not seem to contribute to measurable differences in linguistic knowledge. Whether the child is bright or dull, quick or slow, forward or shy, language is acquired within a short period. But when hearing is impaired, such factors could cause a difference in the way the residual hearing capacity is used.

I should point out here that experts disagree on nearly every topic touched upon in this book. In connection with hearing impairment the chief issues can be grouped around the subject of training residual hearing and the proposed separation of language and hearing. Some people even refuse to use the word *deaf* in their belief that some residual hearing is present in most cases of early impairment. They claim that hearing aids must be applied at the earliest possible moment, certainly before the normal age of the onset of speech. In this way the infant is given the opportunity to make functional use of his residual hearing, which will enable him to acquire language and speech in a normal fashion. If one waits until the infant has passed his second or third year, the child will have grown accustomed to functioning without hearing and will start to use his own nonverbal symbols rather than the verbal symbols provided by society's language. The early massive use of hearing aids would function somewhat like a trigger to sensitize the child to his residual hearing; after this initial push the aid may no longer be needed. In contrast, the later use of the hearing aid encounters what amounts to an atrophy of the unused residual hearing capacity and hence fails.

"But this sounds beautiful," you exclaim. "Why is this not done throughout the country and deafness would be no more!" There is really nothing to argue about, for what I described is not a fact but a theory that could explain the fact if and when it happens. The experts argue much about the facts and only secondarily about the theory. The problem is the difficulty of measuring hearing status: there is simply no automatic, reliable method of doing this at an early age without the voluntary cooperation of the child. Consider what we said about functional hearing —that it is more than a registering of sounds above some given intensity, that it always implies an active processing that gives meaning to the sounds. Thus even if we obtain a reliable reaction to sounds from the infant, this reaction may be a physiological process that could still lack the active psychological aspect that is a prerequisite for human hearing. Also, human infants are notoriously hard to "condition," and many therefore appear to be quite impervious to sound stimulation, although later the evidence points to a normally functioning hearing system. In short, those who have reservations about the indiscriminate use of powerful amplifications point to two difficulties: because reliable hearing measures do not exist for very young infants, the claim that they gained speech and hearing on the evidence of later tests becomes suspect; and hearing amplification may be forced on infants who do not need it, possibly with harmful long-range effects. Some proponents stress the application of electronic devices without going to the extremes illustrated in the first opinion. They believe that not enough auditory training is given to deaf children and thus not enough use is made of residual hearing.

From these observations you should realize that conflicting opinions exist and that you must evaluate each opinion and determine your own position. At the least you should now know that hearing impairment is much more complex than, say, shortsightedness and that a hearing aid cannot be expected to remedy the situation like a pair of glasses. The fact remains that many deaf persons have some measured residual hearing but cannot benefit from a hearing aid, although improved technology and more training might make the wearing of hearing aids more functional in the future.

Let us consider more closely this matter of residual hearing and improved residual hearing. If one must jump over a five-foot hurdle in order to reach a goal, a jump of one foot is functionally equivalent to a jump of four feet eleven inches; neither suffices. This is often the case in deafness. An 80-decibel loss implies much more residual hearing than a 95-decibel loss, but for the purpose of discriminating and processing speech sounds both losses are equally effective. Remember also that a hearing aid cannot selectively amplify only what you want to hear; it indiscriminately amplifies surrounding and interfering noise and can cause discomfort.

I would like to apply similar reasoning to the general category *deaf people* and particularly to such phrases as *the deaf* or *the typical deaf person*. Each person is a unique individual, and innumerable variations in the type, degree, and range of hearing loss interact with the individual personality to produce one individual deaf person. You may have noticed that I try to avoid talking of "the deaf," because although this phrase may be linguistically convenient, it might help to reinforce a false stereotyping that is inappropriate to the occasion and potentially slighting to the individual. Yet while I realize these individual variations, I can still speak of a typical deaf child or of the deaf community. An important common factor combines the members that fall within the extension of these terms: they cannot readily use for communication the verbal language of their society; in fact, most have an inadequate knowledge of the language and consequently use a visible gestural medium of communication. These characteristics are found nowhere but in deaf persons, and they are typical of practically all deaf persons.

These considerations form a natural transition to the second issue on which experts disagree, this time less about facts than about theoretical problems. Again I shall present the argument in its sharpest form to illustrate the points at issue. Some people suggest that the great majority of deaf children who are now at school are not "just deaf" or hearing-impaired; they are in addition, or primarily, language-impaired. This last phrase refers to a neurological deficiency, located somewhere within the brain, that makes it difficult for these youngsters to acquire language. Is there evidence for this opinion? Three assertions are usually made. First, as I have already mentioned, only a few profoundly deaf persons are at home in the English language. Most deaf adolescents leave school with severe deficiencies in the English language, a deficiency that is unknown among hearing persons. The hypothesis of a neurological language deficiency therefore explains the facts rather neatly.

Second, modern medicine has changed the type of children who are now in schools for the deaf. Whereas adventitiously deaf children once were in the majority, today this type of deafness is extremely rare. On the other hand—and this is the crux of the argument—many children who are born with some neurological damage in the speech area of the brain would not have survived in the past; these are now kept alive but eventually are found to suffer from congenital deafness plus other difficulties, notably in the language area. These children are frequently referred to as multiply handicapped deaf or aphasic children, and a few exhibit what is termed behavior disturbances and lack of motor coordination. The argument is advanced by theoretical considerations about the close neurological affinity between hearing and speech and language and the probability that any central nervous damage in the hearing area cannot be confined just to hearing and would spill over into speech and language. It hardly makes sense to separate these areas developmentally either: an infant does not acquire hearing skills in general first, then learn to hear speech sounds, and subsequently obtain knowledge of language and speaking. On the contrary, these processes seem to be organically interrelated.

The first argument is an example of circular reasoning; the second is really no argument at all. Only the third could be a critical issue—but only if audiologists and neurologists could point to an independent neurological measure. In that case some deaf children would be neurologically diagnosed as brain-damaged, and they should have difficulties in language learning; other deaf children would be neurologically diagnosed as intact, and they should do well in language learning. Unfortunately no such neurological test exists, and our knowledge of the etiology of deafness is in most cases a speculative inference from behavioral data, which is not wrong as long as we do not cite the behavioral data as evidence for the correctness of the inference. In short, all three arguments can be highly suspected of circular reasoning and should be met by critical scrutiny.

Of course brain damage does exist among deaf children as among hearing children, and the proportion might be higher, but it is still a very small proportion. The fact remains that the majority of persons in schools for the deaf and in the deaf community are just plain *deaf;* they cannot hear sound, notably the sounds of society's language. This simple fact readily explains the difficulties they encounter with the learning of a verbal language, whereas theories about symbolic defect, language impairment, minimal brain damage, association deficiency, and so on would be hard put to explain the relative normalcy of deaf persons in functions other than hearing.

Now that we have indicated some of the more difficult issues, you will appreciate the need for clarifying the terms we use—for example, *hearing, language, speech,* and *physiological impairment.* A person can be *speech*-impaired, even from birth, without any impairment whatever in his hearing or in his knowledge of language. A person can be *hearing*-impaired but still know a verbal language he acquired before his hearing loss and not be speech-impaired; however, if the hearing impairment is profound, his speech will probably deteriorate without the feedback that hearing provides. A hearing impairment that is profound enough to prevent the hearing of speech with or without a hearing aid is called *deafness.* *Prelingual deafness* makes the acquisition of language and speech articulation very difficult, even though there is no language or speech impairment. In this case we can observe a *psychological* deficiency in knowing the language and in speaking without having to postulate a *physiological* impairment of language or speech. *Postlingual deafness* is a profound hearing impairment after the acquisition of speech.

The discussion in this chapter has thus far evolved primarily around hearing impairment during childhood. This emphasis is not only dictated by the book's aim to fit into a framework of special education but also reflects a state of affairs that sharply differentiates deafness from blindness. A deaf person today most likely lost his hearing early in life, whereas the typical blind person lost his vision during adulthood. Blindness that occurs in childhood is a small proportion of blindness, whereas deafness in childhood is a large proportion of all deafness. Yet even as I say this I should also point out that people's hearing frequently becomes less accurate with increasing age. Hearing loss associated with old age is common but rarely so severe as to constitute deafness; a person suffering this loss is properly called hard of hearing.

We have used the word *language* freely in these last pages, but the meaning of even this word must be specified in order to avoid confusion later. By language I refer to a society's verbal language—English in the United States, Italian in Italy, and so on. Such a language has spontaneously evolved within a society; it reflects the speech used by members of the society, and it is spontaneously transmitted to their children as they hear and speak this language. This is called a child's first language, or mother tongue. It is appropriate to further distinguish between knowing a language and speaking a language. A person who knows a language is one who is "at home" in it, who has implicitly mastered the main rules and the vocabulary that make up the system of the language. This knowledge enables him not only to comprehend and repeat familiar sentences but to comprehend and to produce phrases, sentences, and paragraphs that he has never encountered before.

Consider again that any hearing child who reaches a certain level of development acquires this knowledge as a by-product of living, regardless of the specific society or parental home in which he lives and whatever his intellectual, emotional, or personality characteristics. If we want to understand early profound deafness we must become familiar with this unfamiliar state of affairs: *a deaf child is a human child without a language*.

I have used this or a similar expression many times, and as often as not people misunderstand it because they interpret the word *language* in a different sense from that intended. They object to the phrase *without a language* and argue that even though the deaf child may not speak well by the time he is five years old, he has usually learned ten, twenty, or even a hundred words. To these persons I answer that knowing a language is much more than knowing a limited vocabulary; it is primarily a knowledge of linguistic rules. Other people point to the gestures that a deaf child in a hearing house uses as a spontaneous means of communi-

cation; others refer to the deaf child's play, drawings, and even his everyday activities, through which he manifests an appropriate understanding
of the world. To these objections I repeat that I never intended to include
all meaningful activities under the definition of the word *language*. The
expression does not mean that a deaf child is without symbols, without
communication, without understanding; it *only* means that he is *without
a conventional linguistic system* through which society communicates with
him and he with society.

It is strange that because of this curious misunderstanding I have to
emphasize *only,* as if knowing or not knowing society's language were of
little consequence. Of course language is a symbol, but not all symbols are
language; language is communication, but not all communication is language; language is meaningful activity, but not all meaningful activity is
language. Are these distinctions so obscure or so trivial that they
are hard to understand? Experience has convinced me that there is a deep
underlying reason for these confusions—what in chapter 1 we called a
person's familiar perspective, which is frequently unexamined and un-
articulated. According to this view "language differentiates man from
animal." But what does language mean in this sentence? Nobody asks this
question because it obviously means human language or the speech of
a society. Now when one hears the phrase *a deaf child without language,* it
would follow that this child is not fully human. Because people do not
want to accept this inhuman conclusion, they prefer to change the meaning
of the word *language*. Then they can justifiably reject the phrase as patently
wrong. Is this a semantic confusion or rather a confusion in thinking? The
question will remain with us, particularly when we discuss the deaf child's
intellectual and educational progress.

You have followed the argument thus far and are trying to comprehend
that the phrase *a human child who does not have the knowledge of
a conventional language* expresses the crucial life situation of the prelingual deaf child. You realize too, of course, that reading and writing
are of no use as substitutes for spoken language unless one knows the
language. And you begin to understand how inappropriate it is to compare the reading process of deaf and hearing children, because for hearing children learning to read takes for granted a knowledge of the language; for deaf children learning to read means primarily learning the
language. Now another argument, which you fear may undermine the
entire conception of the deaf child without language, comes to mind.
In the first chapter did we not meet deaf adults who functioned and communicated rather well? They were deficient in their knowledge of the
English language (as indicated by reading or writing), so that their
gestures needed to serve as a functional equivalent of society's language,
but are not these gestures a language?

Here is my reply to this very perceptive question. The gestures that are used in the deaf community are without doubt a human language. In this country deaf people have the American Sign Language, which we shall discuss in some detail presently, but with the exception of the few deaf children born to deaf parents, the vast majority of deaf children are not exposed to the sign language at home and most educational policies, at least until quite recently, have been expressly opposed to it. As a consequence, during the years in which hearing children assimilate the language of their society, deaf children are not exposed to any linguistic system. Because over 90 percent of deaf children are born to hearing parents, the child and the parents manage as well as they can by means of spontaneous gestures that do not go beyond the level of concrete expression or pointing and cannot be called a conventional system. These gestures are of course communication, and they are often symbols, as are play and drawings, but they are not a language in the sense of a linguistic system. The American Sign Language is such a system; it differs from other languages only in that it is not speech.

Even when deaf children come to school and meet deaf peers, they are often left to their own devices and hardly ever encounter the model of an adult deaf person signing. Usually only after a deaf child has been in school for a number of years and is approaching preadolescence will he begin to use freely the sign language of the deaf community. Thus perhaps after age twelve it is no longer true that the deaf person has no language, for by this time the typical deaf child in the U.S. will have acquired a reasonable facility in comprehending and giving conventional signs. Nevertheless, to spend the first ten years of one's life without language and then to use a language for life in the gestural medium is a weighty matter that deserves close scrutiny, if only because it may shake some of our beliefs and assumptions.

The American Sign Language has a fascinating history that links it with medieval Europe and the English-American wars. When the first school for deaf children was being established in the United States it was natural to look to England to learn the special teaching skill through which speech could be taught to deaf children. In the early nineteenth century this skill was still something of a novelty, and the aura of the miraculous surrounded it. Before this time a child born deaf was considered what we would now call totally uneducable; it was thought that without society's speech the dormant intellect of the child could not be awakened. In only a few privileged cases before 1800 were efforts made to raise a deaf child from the level of muteness to speech.

The first school for deaf children was opened to common people in Paris in 1775 by the priest de l'Epée, who adapted for his deaf children many gestures he had observed in Trappist monasteries. (Trappists interpret literally the precept of St. Benedict to keep perpetual silence, and for necessary communication they elaborated a system of manual signs through which they could express their needs and keep in social contact.) Soon schools were opened in other European countries. At that time a young man, Gallaudet, was sent from Hartford, Connecticut, to learn about methods for teaching language to deaf children, but when he arrived in England in 1815 he was not welcome. Whether it was resentment of the recent American Revolution or some other reason we will never know, but this professional secrecy had a lasting impact on American deafness, because Gallaudet proceeded to Paris and became acquainted with the signs used there.

The vocabulary of the sign language has its roots in configurative similarity between the sign and the thing. Thus, because French women around 1800 wore bonnets and men wore caps, the signs for woman and man are respectively a gesture of tying the bonnet under the chin (the thumb of the right hand moves down the chin) or of putting on a cap (clasping an imaginary cap at the right side of the forehead). The same signs also mean female and male. Thus the sign for a little boy is the male sign followed by a sign indicating a low height; a young girl of twelve would be signed by an appropriately greater height after the female sign. Similarly, the words *friend* and *friendship* are signed by putting the two index fingers first one into the other, then the second into the first. If a signer wants to indicate the friend's sex, he simply adds the male or female sign to the friend sign.

From a linguistic viewpoint, the most interesting feature of the sign language is its underlying structure. The language lacks many grammatical features of English—articles, plural, inflection of verbs, indication of verb time. Moreover, sign language leaves out words such as *have* or *is* in sentences like "You have a cold." and "He is anxious," although linguists tell us that many spoken languages do without one or the other of these features without detriment to their communicative and expressive power. A second striking characteristic is the apparent absence of synonyms and gradations in expression. I say apparent because this is not the case for the expert user of the sign language. For example, there is only one sign for happy (imitating the beats of the joyful heart), but the manner in which the sign is made together with the expression on the signer's face and the context of the conversation allows him to express the range from a cool welcome to delirious joy.

A final interesting feature is the dramatic quality of a good signer. If a deaf person tells a story about three persons, like a good stage director he will assign three prominent locations within the range of his signing—for example, person 1 to the left, person 2 to the right, and person 3 in front of his right shoulder. When he says that in a certain club "person 1 borrowed person 2's car but mistakenly thought it was borrowed from person 3 (persons 2 and 3 had identical makes and models but the car belonging to person 2 had a smashed fender) and when person 1 returned the car to person 3, the latter became very angry because he presumed that person 1 had borrowed the car without asking and had smashed the fender, and so on," the good signer would swiftly move or point to the appropriate locations, whereas in English we would have to use cumbersome phrases such as *person 2, the latter, he, his,* or *they* (meaning persons 2 and 3).

Can one thus conclude that the American Sign Language is "as good as" English or another human language? In connection with this question I recall that two hundred years ago King Frederick of Prussia referred to the German language as fit only for peasants and illiterates; he and his court spoke exclusively French. Today we know that there is no such thing as a specific language that can or cannot serve a specific purpose. In other words, the fact that King Frederick considered the German language unsuitable for his status was only an expression of an international fad for imitating the French court and had nothing to do with the German language as such. Similarly, the American Sign Language is most commonly used in everyday social and working relationships, but it also serves effectively in churches for deaf people and in the teaching of philosophy and history at Gallaudet College in Washington, D. C., and it is causing quite a sensation across the country as it is employed by the Theater of the Deaf. (You may have the opportunity to observe this theater group as they interpret drama and poetry that is transcribed from English or original.)

Three final remarks about the sign language are in order. First, it does not lend itself readily to writing, not because of any intrinsic reason but simply because nearly all other writing of language is based on a phonetic-sequential analysis. Second, because the American Sign Language is part of American society and because most sign users are at least somewhat familiar with English, many English words are used when a conventional sign is not available. Third, the American Sign Language also forms part of a rather vague entity to which no name has been assigned but which nevertheless exists and functions—namely, a quasi-natural language of pantomime and improvisation through which deaf people from different nations communicate with each other in rather remarkable fashion. Scholars who are beginning to study the visible communication of deaf people may even conclude that the universal symbolic capacity for acting out is the most basic aspect of the sign language and that it is impossible to distinguish absolutely between natural pantomime and the conventional sign. In fact, sign language as used by deaf people in ordinary life is a dynamic system in which a static single sign out of context has considerable ambiguity. Is it possible that a preoccupation with verbal language in our culture has diminished the ability to use natural gestures among hearing persons? In any case, I have observed deaf people from Italy, Russia, Germany, England and U. S. A. in mutual conversation and have often since wondered whether the divisive curse of the tower of Babel fell on deaf people with less force than on the rest of us "language-wielding" creatures.

In addition to the sign language there is another method of visual communication, and these two "manual" modes should be clearly differentiated. Fingerspelling is not a language in itself but is simply the written English language spelled letter by letter by the shape of the fingers on one hand. You could learn the manual alphabet easily in less than thirty minutes, and you could then spell out words and sentences at a moderate rate. The primary difficulty is reading. To give you a feeling of what it means to comprehend spelling, have somebody read the following letters aloud to you in sequential order: ITISEASYTOFINGER SPELLBUTITISNOPICNICTOREADIT. Fingerspelling is pure English, and thus some educators who are opposed to the sign language are favorably disposed to spelling. (Successful fingerspelling, like writing and reading on paper, obviously presupposes a knowledge of English.) Second, compared to the sign language fingerspelling requires close attention and is potentially stressful. Finally, it lacks the spontaneous dramatic-expressive quality that is part of all human languages. One can say or sign "I love you" or "I hate you" with appropriate tempo, intensity, and bodily emphasis, but it is hard to think how to spell these words and still convey the appropriate emotion.

A word must also be said about speech and lipreading, or better, speechreading. A few—very few—profoundly deaf persons are good lipreaders—that is, they can comprehend what you are saying by watching your face and lips while you are speaking. It is indeed an astonishing feat, and nobody knows what makes a person a good or a bad lipreader. For the vast majority of deaf persons—even those who know language very well—lipreading is at best a hit and miss affair, and mostly it is just impossible. They understand as little from watching lips as you would from watching television without sound. For hard-of-hearing persons, on the other hand, lipreading is a valuable addition to help overcome a partial hearing loss.

The speech of typical deaf people varies from intelligible to unintelligible after you get used to it, to just plain unintelligible. It is an unfortunate fact that most deaf persons have unintelligible speech, so that paper and pencil are the indispensable medium for communication between a deaf person and a hearing person unless the latter happens to know signs or can fingerspell.

By now you should be familiar with the common words associated with deafness, words which have meaning only in relation to the person who is deaf and to those who are near him. You realize now that deafness creates an unusual world and makes us see things in new perspectives.

Differences of opinion exist throughout the entire subject, and we will meet new ones when we discuss the education of the deaf child. However, it is now time to turn to that deaf child and to examine his feeling and his thinking and the reactions of those around him as he grows up in his home and at school.

3

A Deaf Child
Grows Up

By far most deaf children are born to hearing parents. In addition, the sense organ for hearing is not accessible to the casual observer— indeed, it is difficult for the specialist to reach—and deafness does not betray its presence until you speak to the person and wait for a linguistic response. But because we do not expect speech behavior in the newborn infant and because our speech directed to him is usually accompanied by looking and appropriate gestures, the deaf infant may respond quite normally by smiling, struggling, and cooing. This situation results in a unique characteristic of deafness: if the baby is otherwise healthy, deafness cannot be observed in his behavior. It is difficult to obtain a reliable measurement for hearing at a very early age. Pediatricians do not routinely test for it (there is no valid instrument) and often even specialists can only make an educated guess.

Thus the deaf baby is born into a hearing world that does not suspect him of being deaf. He is nursed, he cries and smiles, he is curious and fascinated by moving things and faces, and he responds affectionately to the care and love given him. He begins to crawl and sit up, he handles things and attempts to put them in his mouth, his teeth grow in, he becomes accustomed to eating solid food and to drinking from a cup, he is first unwilling and then quite fussy and insistent about holding the spoon himself. He recognizes persons and things and has his favorite toys and blanket. He toddles and holds on and finally walks around the home and soon outside too. By now he may be eighteen months old and he is a beautiful lovable little boy. The parents dream and talk of his future and their future with him. In retrospect they recall remarks like the following, but at the time they did not feel disturbed about them: "Has he not started to talk yet?" "He must be a late talker, but so was cousin Jean." "Are you sure he can hear well?" "Of course he can hear. See how he runs to me when I clap my hands."

When an adult becomes blind he must go through a process of change, and this readjustment to the losses associated with blindness is so total and so overwhelming that words like *death* and *mourning* are entirely apt, and their manifestations are considered psychologically necessary and purposeful. A good counselor will help the blinded person to work through this period and may attempt to shorten it to a period of perhaps three months, but it would be folly to try to eliminate it altogether. The counselor also knows that as long as the person clings to the hope of retaining what vision he has, the process of death and rehabilitation cannot start.

The parents of a deaf child are in a similar situation. The lovely, healthy, hearing boy has died, and in their acceptance the parents must give birth to a lovely, healthy, deaf boy. The ordeal of the parents is made worse by the often prolonged period of doubts alternating with periods of hope, caused particularly by conflicting opinions among experts. One doctor will say that before the child is three there is really nothing to worry about; another will suggest mental retardation; a third might propose mental disturbance (for example, infantile autism) or brain damage. This happens because the early diagnosis of deafness is a difficult, frequently uncertain procedure. Imagine the fears and unrealistic hopes the parents must endure. If brain damage is proposed, should the parents be thankful that it is *not* deafness? Somehow at this time deafness appears to many parents as the worst of the alternative disabilities. What will deafness mean for the child? You cannot blame parents if at this period the word *deafness* evokes in them a picture of a perpetually dull life of silence, dumbness, inarticulateness, and death. A period of anxiety and personal loss is no time for a realistic appraisal.

This then is a period of great psychological hardship for the parents, a period that can be protracted over months and years due to the uncertainties of the diagnosis. As in the case of blind persons, it is unlikely that parents can constructively accept their child until they are sure of the diagnosis. And opposing views about the training of the child, which we will discuss further, are additional obstacles that parents must overcome to their and their child's satisfaction.

Paradoxically, our deaf boy is blissfully ignorant of any loss and readjustment. In fact, he does not need to readjust. He has now begun to walk and is taking a growing interest in the world around him. His mother —hesitantly at first—accompanies her speaking with gestures. Actually she has done so before, as we all do, particularly when speaking to infants. But now she becomes conscious of making the gestures and of the fact that the gesturing person and not the content of the speech may be the main message that reaches the child. Nothing about this is unusual but the changed awareness on the part of the adult: what counts is not the words but the person who speaks.

Our deaf boy is as keen about pointing to objects and asking for things as any other boy his age. If you asked the parents how they comprehend his wishes, they would refer to natural gestures and the context of the situation. They are satisfied that they can communicate, and the child is also apparently satisfied.

The deaf boy enjoys toys and games. He plays with dolls and blocks quietly by himself or together with playmates. Neither the hearing nor the deaf partner seem aware of or handicapped by the deaf child's lack of hearing and speech. It is amazing how much can be communicated among little children even if verbal exchange is not possible. The deaf boy is not a leader, and particularly when there are more than two children he may get left behind, but this is not a serious obstacle to a generally satisfactory socialization. Also, a somewhat older boy on the block may mother the deaf child.

The parents take their boy along when they shop or take trips of different kinds. They notice that the boy is happy to be exposed to new things and that his eyes are constantly looking for interesting events. The boy's memory is also striking. He notices small changes and points out excitedly the same patterns on different wares. He pays attention to what he and others wear. He loves to look at pictures and is very good at putting puzzles together.

This child does not have at all the withdrawn, silent personality that the parents were afraid would accompany deafness. On the contrary, he is very outgoing and receptive to attention and to signs of affection. In short, his parents have all the evidence they need that their boy is a loving, healthy child, which is reassuring. It helps the parents overcome the initial fears and worries and gives them the strongest possible motivation to accept him unconditionally. If you are ever in a position to counsel the parents of a deaf child, I hope you will at least remember this one phrase: *unconditional acceptance.* My purpose in writing this book is to contribute to this acceptance by helping you to understand realistically the deaf child. Acceptance and understanding go hand in hand, although acceptance can be based on a wrong understanding. In the case of the deaf child acceptance can be based on an understanding that the child will be trained to speak and to use the verbal language. We will return to these assumptions that could hinder full acceptance of the deaf child, but in the meantime, the parents of the deaf boy are wondering about the child's intellectual development. How can the child learn if he cannot hear and comprehend language? Education experts are waiting to tell those parents that nothing is as important for educational progress as language. But before we listen to them, we will observe the deaf child himself. What can he teach us?

We already know about his everyday social activities and we find that he is a normal boy who is interested in what is going on around him. By the time the boy is close to five years old we have had many occasions to observe behavior that manifests an alert intelligence and clever reasoning. When his father watches baseball and football on television our boy often sits beside him. From the game and the reaction of the audience and his father, together with a few gestures, the boy has been able to extract the rules of the game in a rather remarkable manner. The child's knowledge of baseball rules is also demonstrated when he plays a simplified version of the game in the park and obviously understands the rules as well as any other boy. Football of course follows a much more complicated set of rules, but from probing the deaf boy's understanding one can infer that he knows the basic rules of scoring and possession of the ball.

Or take the following incident. Our observant boy is familiar with his mother's shopping habits. He certainly knows how to express his likes and dislikes, and he sees to it that mother buys a big piece of something he likes. One day, as usual, mother selects four sweet potatoes for the family, making sure that the boy gets his own choice of a big portion, because he particularly likes them. While they are standing in line for the cashier, mother suddenly remembers something, motions to the boy to stay with the shopping cart, and goes to get something she apparently forgot. She then returns to the cart with another sweet potato in her hand. Several hours later the table is set for dinner. Our boy helps and on his own adds an extra place setting to the usual four. The mother is genuinely surprised and points to the extra setting with a questioning look on her face. The boy watches his mother's surprise with obvious pleasure. He can guess that his mother would like to know how he heard about the guest for dinner. Like all children, he loves to show off how clever he is. No, he did not "hear" it; he "saw" it when mother went for one more than the usual four sweet potatoes. Was this good reasoning by the child? Of course it was! We may wonder how the child who does not have verbal language can accomplish this.

Before we turn to this exceedingly important problem we might ask: When did the deaf boy reason out the conclusion? It was probably when his mother asked him to wait; he was spontaneously curious and he satisfied his curiosity not merely by taking in information (what?) but by turning it into useful knowledge (what for?). When did he manifest this knowledge? Hours later, when he set the table. Perhaps he could not tell mother earlier for lack of a linguistic medium, but setting the table provided an opportunity for communication which the child used. Undoubtedly the deaf child has a wealth of knowledge, of which only a small part is communicated to an observer. Hearing children also know much more than they verbalize or communicate, but it is particularly important to realize this state of affairs in the case of deaf children.

There is hardly a greater fallacy than the commonly accepted assumption that knowledge, consciousness, and language can be equated. We think that knowledge is found "in books," it is given to us "in lectures," it is planned for us "in curricula." We identify learning with taking in words and memorizing them for a subsequent test situation. We consider action knowing (for example, finding one's way home) as radically different from and inferior to verbal knowing, which is frequently also called abstract knowing. We ask the question "How do you know?" not in the sense of "What are the mechanisms of thinking that bear on this knowing?" but in the sense of "What is the medium through which you know something that is not present to the external senses?" In this view knowledge becomes a problem only when it deals with objects not present to perception; we ask only then for the medium that carries the knowledge of things absent to the senses. For concrete things our answer would be visual images that presumably derive from an original visual perception. But abstract things seem to require a linguistic medium.

If the last paragraph sounds even a little familiar to you—and you could not be a child of our culture without feeling at home in this view—you begin to understand how utterly strange and awesome is the presence of a five-year-old child without a linguistic system. What can be going on in this child's consciousness? What terms does he think in?

A distinguished educator describes the deaf child's world: "He lives in a wordless world. Accordingly, all internal language-clothed thought processes for him are non-existent. All objects at once become nameless and are identifiable only by their most obvious but nameless function. . . . The clock and the calendar are likewise meaningless, for they are but arbitrary indicators of time, an abstraction. Places such as home or grandma's house are without special significance beyond the nameless warmth and affection so evident in such places. . . . His world . . . is a timeless world filled with vague and meaningless comings and goings." After this bleak picture the author continues at once: "The one great and saving grace is the deaf child's intellect which stands as a perpetual challenge to all of us who would bring him to the full realization of his intellectual potentialities." (E. L. Scouten, *Tennessee Observer,* May 1971.) I agree with this sentence wholeheartedly. Because it is the child's intellect that produces thought, identification, abstractions, significance, and meanings, and because the deaf child has this challenging intellect, the aforementioned dismal world is an imaginary creation, a theoretical nightmare built on false assumptions about the nature of knowledge. This is science fiction with a vengeance! Fortunately it does not correspond to any five-year-old deaf child who is alive and kicking in this world.

Do you see what a bad theory can do? These parents have a healthy boy, but the theory tells them that he lives in a meaningless and purposeless world without special significance. We are even more puzzled when we realize that the people who make such statements care for and observe deaf children. Does the children's spontaneous behavior on the playground or in a sympathetic family betray an unorganized, blindly accepted existence that provides no wherewithal for intellectual challenge? How could a deaf child, if he really were so intellectually starved, develop emotionally and socially or even produce anything but an idiot's smile?

Our deaf child's intellect was active, and he applied it to the situation of his mother's shopping. The child *with his intellect* first observed the addition of one to the familiar number of items (not an intellectual accomplishment that can be simply copied and perceived from the environment); subsequently *with his intellect* he arrived at a reasonable conclusion about the purpose of the addition. Hours later he acted according to this intellectual view of his world. Did the boy identify sweet potatoes only by their obvious function? Did the child really have no sense of the time that separated the early afternoon's shopping from the evening dinner? Was his apparent glee in showing off his intellectual feat an unconscious reaction to meaningless comings and goings?

If we want to understand deaf children's thinking we can no longer use the traditional theoretical model of knowing. I know of only one psychologist who deals with intelligence in such a manner that deaf children's mature thinking can be accepted without much ado. For the Swiss scholar Jean Piaget, language does not play a necessary or predominant role in intellectual development as it does in the views of other scholars. I shall attempt to explain Piaget's theory with reference to a normal, hearing child, and you will see at once that the absence of language would be no major obstacle to early normal intellectual progress.

We start with the prelingual period, in which the baby moves around and reaches out for things in a purposeful manner and makes use of various means and activities to obtain the desired end. This is the period of practical intelligence, when to know means practical know-how. We must not conceptualize this knowing as a simple registering of existing cues, because a visual perception of a thing cannot exist without an active organizing on the part of the person of incoming stimulation. Similarly, no simple motoric action, such as handling something or moving around, can occur without an active organizing and coordinating of disparate motoric movements. This organizing and coordinating, which Piaget calls a scheme, is the essential aspect of knowing. A *scheme* is a regulation of action, functioning within the person, that organizes the environment and in doing so puts the person in meaningful (knowing) contact with the environment. In Piaget's terminology a person *assimilates* environmental data to available general schemes and thereby turns these data into psychological content; one can also say that a person *accommodates* available *general* schemes to *particular* environmental data. In sum, schemes are the internal regulations that underlie generalizable actions; *assimilation* refers to the taking in of content to the schemes, and *accommodation* refers to the application of the schemes to content.

Intellectual development consists in the progressive construction of schemes of a higher order through an internal feedback from the actions of the person. This development is not simply an accumulation of new schemes of action (although this is of course included) but it is primarily a qualitative change of the schemes. By living in daily contact with the world, the child organizes his knowing contact with the world in a continuous progression that imperceptibly leads to stages of organization that are qualitatively different from earlier stages. These stages can be considered a general framework or perspective in which the person functions. Intellectual development is the progression from an infant's perspective to the adult's perspective.

Somewhere around the age of one and a half certain behavioral changes begin to usher in a new stage of knowing. Previously knowing was an external know-how, but from this point on two major changes in knowing are slowly being constructed: the child can be in active contact with a thing even if it is not present to the senses, and as a consequence, he can produce symbols. The first point means the beginning of theoretical knowing. Things are not known merely by external reaction but as existing in their own right as objects that are known. As a corollary, the child begins to become aware of his self as the one who knows objects. This awakening to the world of knowable things and the knowing self comes by way of differentiation and stabilization of previous schemes and occurs normally in a deaf child if he lives in an otherwise adequate environment.

The second point—symbol formation—means the child's ability to substitute knowingly something else for an absent thing. The most typical childhood symbolic behavior is play. The child will "play sleep"— that is, he understands what going to bed is and knowingly pretends to go to sleep or plays that a doll is asleep. The child's theoretical knowing of sleep—his scheme of the object *sleeping*—gives the child the means to externalize sleeping in the form of play. In this sense the child's knowing produces the symbol.

External symbols can become abbreviated and internalized. The knowing of a ball may be symbolized by a slight gesture of throwing or eventually by an imperceptible motor or kinesthetic "image." In this theory images—visual, motor, or acoustic—are not faint copies of perceptions which themselves are copies of something outside. On the contrary, the active intellect underlies *all* psychological contact and organizes a perception as a meaningful configuration or an object as something that the person knows or a symbol that stands in the place of something known.

As a consequence, the deaf child, although bereft of a linguistic system, is as yet hardly handicapped in intellectual development. He can know things and people around him, he can produce symbols of play and of fantasy, he can draw and gesture and communicate by actions and gestures. He constantly grows in the understanding of physical and social events. The deaf child's world at age five is very similar to the known world of the hearing child.

Now we must try to understand the role of verbal language—how it functions in development—and relate this to the deaf child's situation. Recall Piaget's notion of assimilation, which is the key concept in his theory. An event does not become a psychological stimulus unless it is assimilated to available schemes. Therefore, a symbolic stimulus has psychological value for knowing only in relation to already available schemes. The verbal language of society does not by itself produce knowledge, but rather must be assimilated to available schemes of knowing. These schemes, I repeat, are neither things nor neurological structures nor images nor symbols; they are general psychological principles of organizing, coordinating, and relating the person within his world.

Verbal language as an entity is of course the product of the thinking persons who compose a society. It is a universal means of symbolizing in the speech medium. It forms a symbolic system that is reflected in the grammar of the language, and it is undoubtedly an important means of human communication. Linguists distinguish language as a conventional symbolic system from symbols that are produced according to individual need, which are called *motivated symbols*. We described such symbols when we spoke of play, gestures, and images. This distinction appears to justify ascribing to verbal language something that other symbols do not have. However, the relevance of this distinction for the growing child is far from obvious or easy to establish, and the mature use of the American Sign Language would make the importance of this distinction doubtful even for adults.

Young deaf children typically develop homemade signs to communicate in their environment. These signs are clearly motivated in that they derive from personal activities or events and may not be meaningful except to people who are around the deaf child. Perhaps our deaf boy made up such a sign for hot—blowing into an imaginary cup—and uses it in connection with hot food (from where it originated), a hot stove, hot water, and even hot weather. In Piaget's terms the boy knows (theoretically) what hotness means and employs a part activity related to hotness as a symbol to communicate hotness. In contrast, a hearing child would be exposed to the English label. He too knows what hotness means theoretically—a precondition for any symbol formation—and assimilates the English label to this knowing, precisely as the deaf boy assimilates a part activity to the same knowing. The knowing is not made better or worse by the assimilation of one or the other medium.

Take the English word *justice*. Does the knowing of this word by itself improve a person's knowledge of what justice means? Of course not. A three-year-old hearing child may use the word, but it will take him close to ten years before he will have a mature concept of justice. Our five-year-old deaf child may use a gesture for fair and just—an important, early-developed notion—and he will also have to wait until adolescence to gain the mature concept.

Language does not provide knowledge, because no symbol, motivated or conventional, can do this. On the contrary, all language and all symbols are meaningful only insofar as they are assimilated to the active intellect of the child. In this sense the meaning of any symbol is totally dependent on available schemes. Literally, the intellect of the symbol-user produces the symbol, and this is equally true for motivated and conventional symbols.

The gesture for hot used by our deaf child originated from the personal reaction of the child and at that time it was motivated. But soon he uses the gesture in different contexts—for example, "Outside hot; I hot"—in which the particular reaction would be entirely out of place. However, this particular gesture happens to be a private symbol that is not part of a conventional lexicon and grammar, and thus its usefulness is severely limited. The hearing child who uses the English word *hot* might also have acquired it in a personally motivated experience, and eventually the use of the word becomes less motivated, but the most important aspect is that the word happens to be part of a conventional lexicon and grammar. By using the gesture our deaf child could communicate to those few who know his private signs; by using this and other English words in various contexts the hearing child not only is able to communicate to all persons speaking English but he also learns a linguistic system.

This then is the main difference between private symbols and society's language: the conventional lexicon and particularly the conventional grammar are present in one but not in the other. This has nothing to do with personal motivation or the alleged superiority of an acoustic speech image over a visual image or a motor image. If our deaf child had been exposed to the American Sign Language he would have learned a different gesture for hot that in its origin was equally motivated—something hot taken from the mouth and dropped. But this sign is part of the sign language lexicon, and in using it and other signs the boy would have acquired the underlying grammar of the American Sign Language.

In chapter 2 we defined language as a conventional system of symbols, which implies that knowing a number of lexical items is not sufficient for knowing a language. A lexicon is of course necessary, but the conventional meaning of a language resides to a major extent in the grammar. The structure of a grammar is not something a child learns as an object of knowing or is even aware of. Nonetheless, this structure is as real as the language itself, and it enables the language to serve as a communicative medium with conventional meanings.

Is the acquisition of a linguistic system a difficult enterprise? We have said that for hearing children it is as easy as being alive. Does one need a special aptitude, a certain high level of intelligence, a particularly motivating environment? You already know the answer. One does not need a special aptitude or motivation, and as for level of intelligence, we can now specify that an infant must have obtained at the least the level of object formation, which is the beginning of theoretical knowing and which makes possible symbol formation. In terms of mental age one could propose a time period of one and a half to three and a half years. This relatively large range shows that individual variations in the acquisition of speech are normal and that factors other than intelligence may play predominant roles. A hearing child two and a half years old who does not yet comprehend or use speech can be adequately mature both intellectually and socially, whereas a child of the same age who does not play or gesture would be somebody to worry about. The first child for some reason has not needed to use speech, but he plays and gestures and is alive and sociable. In a year this child will speak as well as any three-year-old. A two-and-a-half-year-old child's lack of playing or gesturing would indicate a serious deviation from expected symbolic activities, however.

Are play and gestures more important than verbal language? From a developmental viewpoint yes; the active participation of one's own bodily activity appears to be the basic mode of symbol formation, from which all other symbol modes derive. Motor or kinesthetic images, as internalized symbols, are probably indispensable in a way that the better-known visual or auditory images cannot be. If a child who was born blind manifests intellectual deficits at age six, I would be more likely to think that they were caused by the social and emotional attitude of his home than by the lack of visual encounters or images. Parents of blind children are frequently afraid to give the child adequate freedom to explore and handle things and to become bodily involved with the world in which he lives.

Is the acquisition of the lexicon easier than the acquisition of grammar? This is of course an artificial, although quite meaningful, distinction. In the spontaneous acquisition of language these two aspects are tightly interrelated. Obviously children at first do not use words to refer to single lexical items but to stand for actions or events. Later they learn to speak about these things more adequately, and lexical and grammatical know-how can be differentiated. A first answer to the question is that spontaneously one never acquires one without the other. In the artificial learning of a language this question takes on a different meaning. We shall see that deaf children's main difficulty with learning English is its structure or grammar. Many deaf children know a large number of words but do not have the know-how to comprehend or to generate conventionally correct sentences with them. For this reason we are justified in saying that they lack the knowledge of a linguistic system even though they know some words. For the same reason we would not say that an eight-year-old deaf child who has picked up a few conventional signs knows the sign language. What is lacking in both cases is mastery of the linguistic system.

The ease with which a linguistic system is spontaneously acquired by all young children who are exposed to the language is even more remarkable than their learning of the various words or signs within the language. Scientists tell us that the grammar printed in books is only a partial collection of some rules and exceptions and does not at all adequately describe the underlying system of any verbal language. Only a few fragmentary beginnings in this type of investigation have been made for the American Sign Language.

Here then is our language-lacking deaf child, five years old. He does not lack intelligence by which to organize, know, and understand the world around him. He does not lack symbolic skills through which to express this knowing in play, in fantasy, and in gestures. He does not lack communicative skills, because he articulates his knowledge and his desires to others around him by means of pointing or symbols. He does not even lack all conventional symbols, because typically by the time he is five years old he will have established a number of symbols that for him and those who are in contact with him have taken on limited conventional meaning. Indeed, through formal instructions he may already have learned a number of English words. But he does lack a linguistic system and therefore language. In this respect he differs from hearing five-year-old children.

I have questioned the usefulness of distinguishing conventional symbols from motivated symbols, because all symbols derive radically from motivated activity, and any motivated symbol can become conventional whenever the user of the symbol has the intelligence and the need to do so. I also oppose the notion that an acoustic medium is itself superior to a visual medium or that any symbolic medium is intellectually better than another. I do not deny that many aspects of human society would be hard to imagine without a verbal language but merely assert the primacy of the person's intellect over the symbolic medium that he uses. This primacy is itself an intellectual achievement toward which the mature person tends to a greater or lesser degree. (We shall say more on this point when we discuss later developmental stages.) Instead of symbolic differentiations on the basis of origin or medium, deaf children's linguistic lack brings a distinction to the fore that is truly fundamental—namely, a distinction between a symbol that for the user is or is not part of a linguistic system. I would call only a systematic symbol a linguistic symbol in the strict sense; a nonsystematic symbol is a nonlinguistic symbol even though it serves a communicative function or may be a linguistic symbol for another user.

One further remark highlights the deaf child's position vis-à-vis his communicative and other symbols in contrast to that of the hearing child. Where did the deaf child get his symbols? From whatever personal external events *he* chose to adapt for symbolic and communicative purposes. Where did the hearing child acquire his symbols? He also chose many symbols from personal events, but for his communicative symbols he had no choice but to adapt the linguistic symbols provided by society. Linguistic symbols by definition are fully conventional and are handed down by society. The acquisition of the symbols is never a passive or mechanistic paired-associates learning as one often hears; rather, it is an active assimilation. But it is nonetheless the active taking in of something that *is symbolic* in itself, whereas nonlinguistic symbols derive from *real events* that the *person* turns into symbols.

Consequently, in a real sense the deaf child's symbolic life is potentially more independent from outside pressures. For the hearing child linguistic symbols are a challenge but at times also a problem. If you find this difficult to understand consider a trivial everyday example. A friend who is visiting the family proudly presents as a gift some sketches he has made and framed. The parents think the sketches rather poor but politely utter phrases such as "very interesting, hard work, quite beautiful." They even point out the place where the frames might be hung. But after the friend leaves the parents put the sketches away. Their six-year-old daughter, who was present during the presentation, is curious about where the sketches are. She is told that they are not really beautiful and would not look good. Thus she is exposed to contradictory linguistic statements, and she must work out the discrepancy (unless a multitude of similar situations cause her to abdicate critical thinking in the presence of linguistic utterances).

I do not want to stress the potential difficulties inherent in assimilating a linguistic medium in which a full understanding and critical control comes at best only after many years of intellectual development. But I do want to repeat that whatever symbols our deaf boy uses, they are produced by himself and they emanate from his intellectual status and personal needs. This being in control of one's symbols is a factor in the deaf person's self-image that may contribute to his healthy personality development. The absence of a ready-made symbol system perhaps results in some secondary gains for the deaf child's intellect and personality. We must attempt to see these positive factors from the child's perspective if we want to understand and accept the child and his deafness.

4

Education for the Deaf Child

If education is (rightly or wrongly) considered the key to opening up the opportunities of the civilized world to all children, this is nowhere more evident than in the case of deaf children. In fact, to educate deaf children historically meant to literally lead them out of the presumed darkness of a languageless world into the splendid realm of language, where knowledge and a meaningful, civilized existence were to be found. To be deaf has ceased to mean to be dumb (in the sense of stupid), because when deaf people first succeeded in learning society's language people reasoned: deaf people are not stupid because they can learn language. We now think that past societies must have been incredibly prejudiced to link deafness to stupidity, and we consider ourselves enlightened.

But are we really enlightened? People used to say that deaf people cannot learn society's language and therefore cannot be educated and thus are stupid. We say that deaf people learn society's language and therefore can be educated and thus are not stupid. Is there much difference between these views? The reasoning is similar in both cases. And unfortunately, as we have mentioned, the majority of deaf children may not learn the language of society. If we want to dissociate deafness from stupidity we must modify the above statements in important ways.

To state an unpleasant truth is always difficult. Educators are usually so involved with a difficult task that they prefer to focus on individual problems and to rejoice in occasional success. The deaf community is not uninterested, but its opinion is not often solicited. To me the deaf child is an amazing example of human adaptation to a severely frustrating situation. The hearing parents of deaf children are just plain confused, if not brainwashed. What would you say if you had a business that produced, say, radios, and 70 to 80 percent of the products did not work? You would certainly not stay in business very long. But from all available evidence, even a moderate criterion of success, such as a reading level of better than grade four, is only achieved by about 25 percent of all deaf children when they finally leave school after twelve or more years. If anything, this figure is inflated by the exclusion of children who because of suspected retardation and other aggravating handicaps are not admitted to the ordinary schools for deaf children. Additionally, the figure includes postlingually deaf children and perhaps hard-of-hearing cases that should not be classified with the majority of prelingually deaf children. One must add to these considerations the "floor" effect of achievement tests—for instance, on an intermediate battery one cannot get a reading score lower than grade two.

If the criterion of success were speech or speechreading the rate of functional success could be one-tenth that suggested for reading and perhaps one-hundredth for speechreading. In other words, speech and speechreading are not reasonable attainable goals for all deaf children. Yet many people still consider that speech at least is an ordinary achievement of deaf education. Many interpret the statement that deaf people learn language to mean that deaf people acquire speech. Remember that we do not exclude the possibility of success for some individuals. Rather, the thesis I uphold in this book is that all deaf children can learn society's language, not just a minority, but speech and particularly speechreading will always remain a rare skill as little understood as the skill of the creative artist.

First let us take a general look at education for deaf children in the United States. The education of the very young deaf child is usually in the hands of professionals in hearing and speech, who finally diagnose and measure the child's hearing loss. (I say finally to cover the days, weeks, months, and years of frustration that many parents must endure before the presence of a severe hearing impairment is established.) Hearing and speech clinics nearly always have attached facilities to work with children on problems of speech, and they are usually equipped to attack the speech problem connected with deafness before the child is old enough for school. Typically a three- or four-year-old child will spend two hours a day in a classroom where he is exposed to the training of speech and speechreading and to the use of hearing amplification.

Schools for deaf children are either day or residential schools. Many day schools are limited to the age range of a public elementary school, whereas residential schools usually cover the whole age range from kindergarten to high school. With two or three exceptions, every state has at least one public or publicly supported residential school, built to serve the needs of children who lived too far from the school and before local authorities started to provide public day schools in areas of dense population.

Until recently Gallaudet College in Washington, D. C., proudly called itself "the only college for the deaf." Its aim is to provide young deaf men and women who have done relatively well in high school with a liberal arts education. In 1968 a technical college for deaf persons was established as part of the Rochester Institute of Technology, and its popularity among the deaf student body is attested to by an enrollment that in a few years' time equaled the one of Gallaudet College.

Partly due to this elaborate educational setting, which encompasses nearly every deaf child in the country, most deaf young men and women can find constructive work on the labor market and a satisfying social and personal life in the deaf community, a major accomplishment of which everyone has reason to be proud. These positive facts must be kept firmly in mind as we turn our critical attention to the schooling of the deaf child. At the same time, we will have to discover how a school system can fail rather miserably according to its own criterion but by another yardstick can produce a relatively happy and worthy human life.

It is difficult to convey adequately the issues that are implied by the phrase *the oral-manual controversy.* This controversy, which is as old as deaf education, colors all educational considerations; any major decision or change concerning educational practices implies some stand on the controversy. It is much more than a difference in teaching methods; it touches the very core of deaf people's existence. Indeed, in its extreme form oralism is nothing less than the denial of deafness. Its successful application would do away with the usual manifestations of deafness and would produce a person who knows society's language, who speaks the language intelligibly, and who can read this language from the face and the lips of a speaking person. Having then overcome the peculiar handicap of lack of oral communication, the deaf person would feel at home in the hearing society. He would experience as little need for being with other deaf persons as, say, a color-weak person longs for the company of other color-weak persons.

The deaf community has learned to live with the threat of oralism for the simple reason that it is an empty threat. As one deaf adult said to me, "You can cut off the fingers of deaf people and they will sign with their arms, and you can cut off their arms and they will sign with the shoulders." In other words, there is no way to suppress the natural, spontaneous way in which the masses of the deaf population communicate; the singular accomplishment of a few individuals can never become the norm for all.

For a long time the radical opposition between oralism and the deaf community was camouflaged by compromises that pervaded deaf education and by a not-so-benign negligence of the deaf community. A person's training to become an educator of deaf children included hardly any information about the deaf community; books on deafness and the education of deaf persons rarely mentioned the community and its sign language. Hearing parents of deaf children were given no idea that a reasonable alternative to oral education and joining the hearing society was available.

The compromise in education took the following form: oralism strictly prevailed in all formal teaching, but outside the classroom and for functionally useful and necessary information a manual mode of communicating was permitted. This double standard created no problem in a day school, where nearly all activities are classroom activities, and thus day schools were typically "pure oral" schools. Rather, this compromise evolved in the residential schools. At the oral extreme, four or five private residential schools considered themselves pure oral and officially rejected the compromise with manualism. They prohibited signing. If a child relapsed into signing too frequently or if he failed to make reasonable progress in oral education, he was dropped.

However, the vast majority of schools, including the public residential schools, used oralism in the classroom and permitted manualism outside the classroom. This tacit permission was a point of contention for many teachers who adhered to the oral ideal, but for practical purposes there really is no choice when, for example, seven-year-old Susan has to be told that her father would pick her up five hours later than usual because his car broke down some two hundred miles from the school. If no pantomine or gestures are used, such a simple message becomes an almost impossible task.

Imagine this child in a pure oral school. Susan is getting ready for her departure when the messenger arrives, shaking his head (not even oralists completely give up the natural gesturing that accompanies ordinary speech). The girl is placed in a favorable position for speechreading and the messenger begins slowly: "Father phoned. His car broke down. His car is broken. He will not come now. He will come in five hours, after dinner." The child stares at the face of the speaker. Fortunately for her she noticed the speaker's "no" gesture, and putting two and two together, she guesses that something has delayed her being picked up by daddy. Thus, guessing correctly the word *father,* Susan smiles happily during the remainder of the message. She has already learned, as all deaf pupils quickly learn, to be satisfied with a facsimile of listening, because if she started asking "What did you say?" and "Repeat, please" after every word she did not understand, the situation would become unbearable, especially for the hearing speaker. And he would soon show his frustration to the deaf child, with the result that both the speaker and the child would become unhappy. It is much easier to simulate intelligent listening, to smile and to receive a smile, and to have done with. After all, it is not vital for Susan to know the exact reason and length of the delay; she is as capable as any other child of imagining possible reasons, and later she can compare her anticipations with the facts that she observes.

In other than pure oral schools the house parent would relay the message by spelling or signing that would include the pantomime of driving a car and pointing to the watch and the hour of the father's expected arrival. As the deaf child grows older and communication of messages becomes somewhat more important and details cannot be left to intelligent guessing, with a few exceptions, only the manual method is convenient and inspires reasonable confidence in the speaker and the receiver that the message has been transmitted.

The pure oral schools used to call these other schools manual schools in an unambiguously pejorative sense, and these other schools strenuously defended themselves against this charge by pointing to the official curriculum, which was entirely oral. This defensive attitude only played into the hands of the oralists: these schools embraced oral education in theory but demonstrated in practice that this education did not work outside the artificial setting of the classroom.

A second compromise became quite common in residential schools. You have probably guessed already that the designation of usual class grades is quite meaningless with deaf children. A six-year-old hearing child who has as an educational objective the task of mastering successive reading levels is of course highly skilled in his native tongue; he knows his language. Grade and reading levels correspond easily, at least in the elementary school and for the traditional middle-class milieu. But even if the deaf child should master reading level one, he can in no way be put on a level with a hearing child who finished grade one. Therefore, schools for the deaf wisely avoid sequential class designation from grades one to twelve and instead make rough divisions according to age: the primary division, from age five or six to age ten or eleven; the middle division, to age fourteen or fifteen; and the upper division, to age eighteen or twenty.

In many schools the primary division was rigidly separated from the higher division, one reason for which relates to the oral-manual controversy: the young deaf child was in this way less likely to come in touch with a person who knew and used the sign language. Moreover, by the time of the middle division the nonselective schools could no longer continue for all pupils the pure oral education that had been maintained for the preceding five to seven years. In this way, another use of signing was introduced, this time in the classroom proper, but it was limited to pupils who by their past performance could not reasonably be expected to benefit from the further use of the pure oral method. In other words, a kind of track system evolved by necessity. Many schools had manual and oral divisions for the older students, and these two divisions were often equated with a vocational program for the majority and an academic program for the minority, some of whom would then proceed to Gallaudet College.

In the manual division signing was thus more or less officially permitted. I say more or less because the oral ideal was still so pervasive that manualism was even then permitted only as a last resort. The schools argued—and rather convincingly, one must admit—that these children had been exposed to the learning of English by the oral method for a long time and had not acquired sufficient linguistic knowledge for practical use. Now they were twelve years old, and if the school was to teach them any subject matter beyond Jack and Jill, it had to stop concentrating only on the English language and communicate the topic in a way that would be comprehensible to these deaf youngsters.

A second reason for this compromise was less openly admitted. We mentioned that an effort was made to keep young deaf children away from people who knew the sign language, but in practice this goal could not be completely accomplished. Occasional deaf youngsters came from deaf families; the child came in contact with some deaf adults at school; and there were older deaf brothers or sisters and contact with the deaf community outside school. In short, by age twelve the need for a functional way of communicating had become so great and so much educational frustration had built up that the sign language of the deaf community could no longer be kept from the deaf students.

Thus in the combined method of the upper school you would find deaf adults who were teaching geography or science. Teaching still took place largely in the English language, but while the teacher spoke he simultaneously signed. This simultaneous method is the same as a simultaneous translation of one into another language: the face and the lips "speak" English, the fingers and the arms "speak" sign language. Gallaudet College is the foremost user of this method, which assumes that its user knows both languages and that the prime function of sign language is to make lipreading less of a guessing game. But when this method is used in the classes of schools for the deaf, this assumption is clearly unfounded. The deaf adolescents have only a limited knowledge of English, and for them the purpose of the method is not just to make lipreading easier but to convey information through signing and to continue providing an opportunity for learning the English language.

In fact, the English language is the main subject throughout all the years in school, and as long as public education remains what it is, this goal is not likely to change. In public schools for hearing youngsters reading is still the number one criterion of scholastic success, at least for the first six years of school. Because the child knows a language, one could conceivably entertain the notion that other mental activities would be equally or more important and worthy of being stressed for the hearing child. But for the deaf child, it seems inconceivable even to compare any other educational activity as equally or more worthwhile. In short, the users of the combined method, like the proponents of the oral method, had one principal aim: the teaching of the English language. In this sense the methods are indistinguishable in their goals and educational priorities.

In the early 1960s, when Russian achievements in space flights provided the impetus for reappraisal in all fields of education, reports began to come to the United States about the introduction of fingerspelling into the early education of deaf children in Russia. The reports mentioned dissatisfaction with the achievement level in reading, and because the purely oral method of speech and speechreading appeared to be an inadequate basis for the acquisition of language, fingerspelling was proposed as the means by which to overcome this deficiency. Fingerspelling makes each letter clearly visible and therefore can take the guesswork out of speechreading.

Fingerspelling was of course known and used in the United States, but until recently only one school, in Rochester, New York, employed it consistently in education, and by 1960 even there it was introduced only in middle school. After hearing about the Soviet decision, several schools adopted fingerspelling for even the youngest children, but it is still too early to evaluate the educational impact of this method. Two things stand out in this effort toward improving teaching methods. First, because achievement is generally so low, it would be difficult to think of a method that could do worse than the present one. I do not mean to be flippant, only to convince the hesitant that in this situation any reasonably motivated change is potentially better than no change. Oralists have been fond of using the counterargument that a simultaneous use of the manual mode would take away from the young deaf child the incentive to accomplish the admittedly arduous tasks of speechreading and speech. "Every child must be given a fair chance of oral education," went the slogan. "Only if the child shows absolutely no aptitude for oral education can manual education be permitted." From this sentiment flowed the second compromise mentioned above—the official policy in most public residential schools of providing no alternatives to a purely oral education for the first six years and of permitting a manual method only after clear failure. The fact that this strategy condemns the vast majority of deaf children to become scholastic failures does not seem to shake the oralists from their missionary zeal; on the contrary, they blame inconsistency in oral education and point to the first compromise, the manual permissiveness of the residential schools outside the classroom. In this atmosphere no innovation could possibly be accepted, because sooner or later some influential parent would complain to the legislature that in the publicly supported school his child is not being given a fair opportunity to become like hearing people.

The introduction of early fingerspelling has broken the ice; educators now dare to speak of the masses of failures. They speak out against the unreasonableness of a method that assumes an exceptional talent. The deaf child finds that education is meeting his needs halfway. Fingerspelling is still not the ordinary language of the deaf community, but at least it is English that is made visible to the eyes of deaf persons in a way in which speechreading can never be. In this sense the educational process began accepting deafness, and this is perhaps the most significant effect produced by the general interest in fingerspelling.

Another recent change in general attitudes, this time toward minorities in general, has had a profound influence on the education of the deaf child. The general public has become interested in the deaf community and in its language. For the first time scientists consider it appropriate to study the deaf community, and linguists take the sign language seriously. When the black or the Puerto Rican child was not merely permitted but was encouraged to use his own customs and language in school, educators of deaf children almost naturally began to do the same with their pupils. No longer are deaf children viewed primarily as children who must be made as nearly as possible into hearing, middle-class adults. Spokesmen from the deaf community and concerned parents find that their voices are being heard.

If ten years ago someone had suggested the possibility that a state school for deaf children would officially and openly accept the full scale of manual modes of communication without any reservation whatever, he would have been dubbed an unrealistic dreamer. But in 1969 a large residential school for deaf children, the Maryland School in Frederick, adopted what they called a program of "total communication." (Other schools are now adopting similar programs.) This program implies that communication is valued above any specific method of communicating. It tells the deaf child as soon as he enters school that communicating is the main task of the school, and it encourages him to learn the full range of communicative media available.

This program is decidedly not against speech or the English language. It urges the use of hearing amplification and of speech, but it does not wait until the child fails before encouraging other ways of communicating. It goes along with the child's natural gestures and pantomimes. It welcomes homemade signs that can perhaps be understood only by others in the school, as in the hearing world a troup of scouts may have a few "private" words comprehensible only to members of the group. Because this program was organized in cooperation with the deaf community, the American Sign Language is an acceptable visual language to which the young deaf child is exposed. Fingerspelling is also an indispensable part of the visual language, if only to spell proper names or to designate concepts for which a sign is either nonexistent or unknown.

As its name implies, the total communication program expects from its participants a total commitment to communication as an overriding good that must be fostered by all possible means. Consequently, there is no room for "purism"—neither speech nor English nor even sign language can become an educational object in itself. Moreover, the program requires the full participation of the family. It encourages the parents of deaf pupils to acquaint themselves with the deaf community and its sign language, thus giving the parents realistic perspectives and expectations and enabling them to communicate articulately with their deaf child. In the past many parents were given no guidance or encouragement to benefit from the available sign language of the deaf community. I recall the mother of a sixteen-year-old deaf girl who bitterly complained to the school psychologist who mentioned the sign language: "Why did you not tell me of it ten years ago when the girl was small and still close to me? Now we have grown so far apart she cannot articulate what she thinks or feels. I cannot communicate with her and stand by like a passive on-looker." This girl went through a severe identity crisis; she did not feel comfortable either in English—she was at a typical third to fourth grade reading level—or in sign language. And this happened in a school that oralists used to refer to as manual.

At the turn of the century when oralism became the official educational policy, the deaf community, who were given no voice in the framing of the policy, stated defiantly: "Whoever is against the use of a visual-manual mode of communication is not a friend of deaf people." They said this not because speech and speechreading are not desirable but because a policy of oralism excluded and prohibited a manual mode of communicating. Now the situation is changing; for the first time schools are beginning to accept the deafness of their children. This is therefore an exciting time of constructive innovation from which the practitioners of education for nondeaf students can also learn many useful lessons. As other schools adopt total communication—and the indications are that many will do so within a few years—an open and responsive atmosphere will prevail, in which scientific opinions—or in the absence of them, at least common sense—have a chance to be heard and put into practice.

I believe that a school system should be judged by its failures, not by its successes; it does not take great teaching talent or special methods to educate the gifted child. If I seem to be overly hard on oralism, I make no apologies. In subsequent chapters I will present scientific and psychological evidence which I believe will prove the basic assumptions of the oralists wrong. But an educator is more than an applied scientist; he must also be a responsible adult who cares for the person within the child. As a human being and an educator, I am impatient with and appalled at an educational policy that not only does not produce what it promises—except in a few privileged cases—but that also implies an untold amount of failure and misery for deaf children and their parents alike. I am happy that the ice is broken, and I look forward to the day when the oral-manual controversy is but a chapter in the history of deaf education.

The main difference between the traditional oral method of education and the method called total communication is that in the traditional curriculum the child must do what the teacher wants him to do, whereas in total communication the teacher is attuned to the child's own spontaneous expressions. Language drill, speech drill, and lipreading drill are the main activities of the young deaf child in a traditional classroom; the child regurgitates the linguistic patterns that the teacher imposes on him. There is no denying that some teachers are amazingly inventive in making the language exercises interesting and exciting to the children, but in the final analysis they are still rote exercises, and no living, generative language can be acquired in this manner. Further, in this setting all topics tend to take on the character of speech drills. Whether the subject is mathematics or geography, the medium of the verbal language becomes the focal point and the stumbling block, and the substantive knowledge of mathematics or geography is not communicated.

In contrast, total communication emphasizes the spontaneous expressions of the child. A young deaf child spends a great deal of time in "conversation periods." Any good teacher will argue that this method is not new and that spontaneous expression is certainly encouraged in any good oral education. The difference is the fact that in traditional teaching the only permitted method of expression is the correct English language and speech, of which the child has mastered only a few words and phrases. By necessity, therefore, the child's spontaneity is severely restricted. In total communication the child expresses himself primarily in sign language; these manual and visible instruments are recognized as the normal means of communication for a person whose hearing is not functionally intact.

However, the point is not to teach sign language but rather to use the spontaneous communication of signing to encourage a two-language communicative exchange. For this purpose the teacher reflects the child's own expressions to provide informal occasions for spontaneously improving these expressions; he will sign back to the child in a more adequate manner, and he will accompany all signing by English speech. Exactly the same thing is required of the child's parents; their active cooperation is an integral part of this program.

In a short time the young deaf child acquires this method of communicating by spontaneous imitation. During the conversation periods the child focuses primarily on what interests him. The school atmosphere is not centered on language but on the child's communicative interest; language learning per se is considered too narrow an educational goal. This is really the only psychologically sound way to acquire a language, particularly a first language—not by formal learning but by informal imitation, an unconscious discovery of general linguistic rules, and the spontaneous desire to communicate.

The fact that deaf adults were included in the formulation of the school program of total communication ensures, among other psychological benefits, that the child's model is a natural, viable method of communicating. Educated deaf adults agree that the most natural and comfortable way to make themselves understood is by the simultaneous use of signing and speaking. In short, instead of the manual and verbal modes of communication opposing each other to the detriment of better communication—as is so often the case in traditional schools—they are constructively used to reinforce each other.

The reader may recall that we considered the teaching of the English language to be the principal aim of both the oral and manual methods. What seems to be new in total communication is not merely a shift in method but a shift in aim. Perhaps the persons who conceived the program could not or did not want to articulate this major shift, and at this point I do not wish to dwell on it but merely to make you aware of the change. What does total communication imply as far as the educational objective is concerned? Perhaps total communication is not really an objective but an atmosphere, a general setting in which education takes place—just as society's language is a pervasive part of the environment in which the hearing child develops. What then is the educational goal, or what should it be? At least a tentative answer must be given to this question, and we shall return to this point in the last chapter.

5

From School
to Adulthood

How does the profoundly deaf child develop socially, emotionally, and intellectually in the conflicting atmosphere of uncertain educational goals? What happens to him when he leaves school? The truism that each child is different and that each child's home and school situation is different is even more applicable to the child with a disability than to the average hearing child (the norm). From what you have already learned about conflicting expert opinions in diagnosis, auditory treatment, educational policies, and attitudes toward the deaf community, you can estimate the variety of external, frequently conflicting pressures to which the deaf child is exposed. What would be considered an abnormal array of frustrating circumstances in the case of hearing children frequently is the norm for deaf children.

Experts disagree about the value of residential versus day schools. (Although we mentioned several controversies, we barely touched others.) The most heated arguments are primarily derived from the oral-manual controversy; however, an important consideration in favor of the residential school is the opportunity it provides for the deaf child's socialization. At least until now the majority of deaf adults have developed their sense of belonging to and being at home in society through attending a residential school during childhood and adolescence.

This should not be surprising. Deafness is a very big obstacle to communication, and the greatest psychological danger to which the deaf person is prone is isolation. In the hearing and speech clinic social contact with other deaf children may be very limited, particularly if speech is the only activity that is openly encouraged. It is usually at school that a deaf child meets another deaf child for the first time. And who can fathom what happens to the child's view of himself and his world when he first comes to a residential school and finds himself surrounded by a crowd of other deaf boys and girls. The process of socialization is psychologically so vital that even if none of these children had ever communicated by signing before, the mere fact that they are together ensures that spontaneous gestures, pantomime, and soon homemade conventional signs develop. In this spontaneous activity the children are largely left to their own devices. Since deaf children are generally unfamiliar with common, culturally transmitted games and lack the skills of organizing rules for games, their play in primary school takes on a roughhouse character that strikes the observer as decidedly immature. But by and large these children manifest patterns of social interaction, friendship, play, and games that are similar to those of hearing children.

This relatively simple adjustment may seem surprising because at least in our society a residential school setting for children as young as five is clearly unusual. And indeed, for almost all hearing children such an arrangement would be considered highly unsuitable for psychological adjustment. The case of the deaf child is unique, however. The school offers him a natural entrance to the deaf community, within which the child will eventually find his psychosocial adjustment. And unless the deaf communities themselves build and staff schools and recreational facilities, the residential schools provide the only comparable alternative.

When you talk to deaf adults you are impressed by their attachment to their schools despite continuous failure experiences in education. To them school really became a second home, a place where they found and accepted themselves, first as deaf boys or girls and finally as adults. We must remember that a prelingual deaf child does not at first experience his poverty in speech and language as a handicap. His entrance into a school for deaf children around age five or six comes just in time to help him avoid the potentially crippling experience of the communication handicap.

At the age of early elementary school awareness of self is only dimly articulated. A seven-year-old deaf child is not consciously aware of his deafness. The adult world is full of mysteries, of incomprehensible events and rules that any child, hearing or deaf, simply accepts the way one accepts the arbitrary rules of one's language or one's attire. For the deaf child the face- and lip-moving world of speech is simply another mystery, a reality that he neither emotionally nor intellectually assimilates. If he could verbalize he would truthfully say that it does not bother him at all.

To meet and live with other boys and girls whose activities can be much more fully accepted than those of hearing children must be a tremendously meaningful experience for the deaf child. In contrast to hearing boys and girls he may have known at home, here are boys and girls that he can "make real" and "make sense of." Together these children can construct the kind of social relationships that are common among all children of a similar age. We have remarked that socially these children are left to themselves, perhaps to a much greater degree than typical hearing youngsters. They are not handed down a rigid tradition of verbal mores. Certainly the children are confined within a school discipline, but this mainly regulates their interaction with the hearing world. Just as the deaf children must "invent" their first conventional signs for communication, they also "invent" social norms for playing and living together. This setting creates a social and affective independence, a sense of relying on themselves that characterizes deaf adults, in notable contrast to other disabled persons.

How does this affect the child's relationship with his own family? On this point it is impossible to generalize because the degree and quality of a deaf child's acceptance at home varies tremendously, but this much can be said. First, most deaf children adjust remarkably well to residential school and despite their young age soon show happiness when mother takes them there. Second, the social acceptance and the sense of reality are factors of psychological strength and vitality that can only contribute positively to the child's life in his natural family. If the child's attachment to his parents is strained or barely existent, this new experience is even more important for the child's psychological health.

Paradoxically, although the school provides adequate opportunities for early social and emotional development—simply by permitting socialization and cooperation in a relaxed atmosphere—the same can hardly be said for intellectual development. Instead, most schools insist on what from the deaf child's perspective is a mystery of the adult world: speech that cannot be heard and language that is supremely arbitrary. Unfortunately for this educational objective, most deaf children accept this insistence on speech with the same indifference that characterizes any child's exposure to something he cannot understand and cannot alter. This "lack of motivation" is the bane of conscientious educators, who become considerably more frustrated than the child. In the child's view, his reaction is simply a natural continuation of much that has gone before. To think that the child will have a natural need for learning language at this age is a psychological misunderstanding about the role language plays in early development.

From the age of two, when his knowledge moved beyond the level of immediate reaction to present events, our deaf child expanded his world of knowing and produced external gestures or internal images as he needed them. When he meets other deaf children, he has the exhilarating experience of constructing new and meaningful ways of relating to others at the same time that he expands his skill in communicating. His mental development is at the threshold of what Piaget calls the stage of concrete operations. From two to six years of age he elaborated the first stable concepts or frameworks within which he can know the world, and now he is ready to apply his knowledge. Typical concrete operations are classification, seriation, and quantification or numbers. (Piaget calls them operations in the sense that action is internal and no longer simply external.) Thus a deaf child can comprehend that there are more plants than flowers and that one's uncle can be younger than oneself and that $162 + 73$ is the same as $160 + 75$. He comprehends it even though he may not be able to verbalize it and he may not have been told these particular facts. He has within him his own criteria of comprehension—the framework of concrete operations which he can apply to these and other types of problems.

The next chapter will discuss ways in which we can observe these concrete operations whether the child possesses the skill of a conventional language system or not. In fact, without considering the confirming case of deaf children, Piaget concluded that the operations of thinking are actions (or better, regulations of actions) that have nothing to do with language or symbols. In any case, symbols, including language, are used in the service of thinking schemes; they should be considered the product and never an explanation of thinking.

The language and speech exercises of the traditional curriculum provide scant nourishment for the budding concrete operatory intelligence of the young deaf child. The teacher may have been taught and may honestly believe that in teaching language she is giving the deaf child the wherewithal to organize and "intellectualize" his knowing. She cannot understand why the deaf child is not eagerly taking in and making use of this precious tool. But as we have said, deaf children are the best witnesses that language is not an indispensable means for early intellectual development. However, mental capacities need nourishment, and every child thrives on environmental and social encouragement. Many families of deaf children are not inventive enough to find other than verbal—and there are many—means of communication. They give the child warmth and affection, but they do not understand how to provide an atmosphere conducive to intellectual growth. The ambiguous and conflicting counsel of experts has undoubtedly contributed to parents' inability to accept fully the deafness of their child and to make sensible provisions to meet his needs. Deaf children commonly spend a good part of their waking hours in front of a television that is blaring away at full volume, thus giving the child, if not sound, at least the sense of vibration together with the visual display. This is an intellectually sterile occupation for any child, and it can only be more so for the deaf child.

Unfortunately, the typical residential school offers no radical improvement in the intellectual atmosphere. At a younger age limited experience might have a slight depressing effect on intellectual development, but a similarly restrictive experience has more serious and long-lasting effects on a child of elementary school age. Research findings on the intellectual functioning of deaf children and adolescents (discussed in detail in the next chapter) point to a slight, practically negligible lag at middle childhood, ages six through ten. But in formal thinking, which begins to develop at preadolescence, the differences between mean performance levels of deaf and hearing persons are large and are symptomatic of a less mature style of thinking. This retarded development is caused by the impoverished intellectual situation in which deaf children live during the years of early school.

Lest you think that lack of language is the factor principally responsible for the developmental lag, I hasten to add that research has demonstrated remarkable similarities in overall intellectual development between deaf children (who have no language) and hearing children from disadvantaged social or physical environments (who have language). These disadvantaged children also suffer principally because neither home nor school encourage their thinking abilities. The school's insistence on the arbitrary norm of reading achievement causes the disadvantaged children to experience failure and at the same time withholds from them opportunities for exercising available thinking capacities.

The language failure of the deaf child is immeasurably more severe than the reading failure of many hearing youngsters, who at least know language orally. But precisely for that reason the hearing child experiences scholastic failure in quite a different way: he readily equates failure with rejection by the society that was already believed to be responsible for the initial disadvantaged condition. Thus, the early failure is a tragic event that has untold repercussions for the affected hearing child, not the least of which are the missed opportunities and unused challenges for intellectual development.

Scholastic failure has none of these harmful consequences for the deaf child. Because he does not know what verbal language is about, does not feel a need to use it for everyday living, is strong in the newly discovered skills of social relations and communication to other deaf children, the deaf child literally does not know what he is missing. What is the evidence for this strange assertion? The hearing child who consistently fails in school, eventually becomes a behavior problem—an emotionally crippled child, a drop-out, a delinquent; he simply cannot take it. In contrast, the deaf child fails for three, six, nine, or twelve years and emotionally and socially he is none the worse for it. Where, the observer asks, does he get the remarkable resilience to withstand so much frustration? The answer must be that the objective situation simply is not as subjectively frustrating to the deaf child as we would expect it to be to hearing children. In addition, this reaction, or rather, this lack of reaction, provides an early clue about the attitude that deaf youngsters develop toward the hearing world.

When the linguistic structure is limited to subject-verb phrases of the simplest type, one can hardly expect that the content of the language lesson will challenge the child's thinking capacity. Language, reading, and speech are of course the main part of the deaf child's ordinary curriculum. Even where it goes beyond—notably in mathematics but also in subjects like geography, government, and history—the traditional emphasis on the verbal medium heavily influences the teaching procedure; here too knowledge of language is considered a prerequisite. All school subjects turn into language lessons and become occasions for showing how little linguistic skill deaf children have rather than occasions for showing how intelligent deaf children can be.

By the time deaf children are in middle school some practical activities are added to the curriculum. Cooking, carpentry, painting, book binding, the use of simple electronic machines, and many other skills—in fact, a rich variety of everyday and occupational skills—are typically taught in these schools. These courses are meaningful to the young girls and boys; they are popular and usually no stigma is attached to them as being not academic or fit only for students who are scholastic failures. The activities make school more bearable for both the teacher and the student. It was there that the schools first permitted the use of manual communication to supplement the lack of linguistic knowledge.

There is reason to believe that the deaf adolescent undergoes the psychological change from childhood to adulthood with less uncertainty and fewer emotional problems than his hearing peers. Many hearing youngsters go through an identity crisis that can last for years, whereas the deaf child has been working his way toward this crisis from the day he started to think of himself, and he is better prepared for an adequate response. Of course this seeming psychological advantage comes at what would seem to us the cost of a severe restriction in intellectual and social outlook. In this sense the world of the deaf adolescent is simpler and less subject to upsetting and unsettling contingencies than the world of the hearing teenager.

If the main task of adolescence is acceptance of self as a responsible and worthwhile person, the deaf young person must consciously accept his deafness with all the limitations it entails. At this age a deaf youngster can see that he lacks something that other people have. A deaf boy may begin to realize that some occupations are excluded from his vocational choice. A deaf girl may become aware that a variety of tempting social settings are but fantasies that must be subordinated to reality. Each deaf adolescent must experience a crisis and accept his deafness, at which point he becomes a full member of the deaf community, because for the vast majority of deaf adolescents acceptance of deafness means affirmation of belonging to the deaf community.

The deaf youngster is usually well prepared for this life choice. When he was six years old and first mixed with other deaf children, when he learned to enjoy pantomiming and gesturing, when he discovered his own powers of thinking and communicating, he was already well on the way toward the choice he would one day make on the threshold of adulthood. He is now fifteen years old and has spent ten years in an educational setting where the official message was "Learn society's language and society will accept you." We have tried to indicate that the deaf child never accepted this message because it did not make sense to him intellectually or emotionally. Thus from his first exposure to this policy he devised a strategy to deal with it. Perhaps it can be called a defense mechanism. The important thing is that it kept him emotionally healthy and strengthened his ego. He would not be seduced by the school's message; he would not internalize it. If he had he probably would have become an emotional cripple filled with feelings of failure and guilt. Even worse, he could have become an isolate who belonged nowhere.

What fantasies, dreams, and ideals fill the deaf adolescent? How is his self related to these symbolic constructs? First, in comparison with his hearing peers, his symbolic life is bound to be simpler and less rich; second, it is more reality oriented; and finally, it is firmly anchored in the self. If you can imagine removing verbal language as a source of symbolism—take away the themes, the ideals, the fads that society talks about; take away the verbalized advertisements, political slogans, racial prejudices, religious creeds; take away the easy-going manner of small talk; take away the tales and legends, the songs and poetry, because hardly any of this becomes part of the deaf child—you will realize that much less is imposed on the deaf child than on the hearing child. And here is the contradiction of the deaf person: he is poor in symbolism, but he is free from imposed beliefs; he has a restrictive simplicity on the one hand and ego strength on the other hand.

This "advantage" of deafness is most conspicuous during adolescence, from which most deaf adults emerge with no resentment, with no unrealistic goals, with a healthy degree of personal pride and independence, and with a feeling that they do not owe overly much to the hearing society. They do not feel discriminated against because theirs is a voluntary, sensible choice based on a realistic appraisal of their communication condition. Pride in belonging to a minority group is rarely free from a bitterness because the majority created the minority problem, but pride in belonging to the deaf community is primarily an affirmation of self and a healthy defense against isolation.

If you ask a deaf adult whether he wishes above all else that he could hear, he will find the question as meaningless as whether he wishes to have been born a hundred years ago. For the deaf person, deafness does not imply that something was taken away from his self. On the contrary, it is part of his self; if he were not deaf, he would not be himself. Such reasoning might sound strange to our conformity-loving ears, but it should help us realize that early profound deafness is not a problem that the afflicted person works to overcome but a condition he accepts. Of course deafness is never good, but deaf people, even those whose early education pushed them as much as possible away from the deaf community, often demonstrate remarkable capacities to adjust to it.

Apart from the few deaf persons who continue education at college, deaf young men and women enter the labor market and usually have little difficulty finding a job. Surprisingly, verbal language is not a vital part of many jobs, at least not in low-level occupations. The participation of deaf persons in better paying, high-level occupations is much less frequent, however; this alarms many people, particularly because manual labor is increasingly being taken over by machines.

In the social sphere deaf people often live amazingly active, outgoing lives, a situation that is easily understood when one remembers their restricted inner, symbolic lives. They are extroverts—fond of meetings, picnics, outings, clubs, gossip, and travels. The sign language is their medium of communication; without it their lives would be unthinkable. They have very few intimate contacts with hearing persons and usually find all they need within their community: companionship, friendship, love, marriage, amusement, recreation, sport, religion.

Everything we have said about the profoundly deaf person was calculated to help you see his life from his own perspective. To the hearing person deafness is a strange, different world. A person who hears may well believe that the deaf world is very restricted, that deaf people miss so many things. But the hearing person has developed different capacities and has had different experiences. It does not make sense to judge another person's life by a perspective in which he does not participate. If you would help the deaf person you must start with what is positive and strong in him; you must not impose an alien or unattainable goal on him. For too long experts have determined to know what is best for the deaf child and adult without taking into account the real-life situation. In the case of the deaf person the existing deaf community, with its social and linguistic customs, is of overriding importance. By all means let us try to improve the deplorably low academic achievement, the failure to learn the English language, and employment at relatively low levels. But we must at all costs avoid even the appearance of depreciating solid achievements, such as normal intelligence, the functional utility of the sign language, and the practical absence of unemployment.

The picture of the deaf person's situation presented here is typical for the American scene, although it obviously cannot do justice to many individual differences. Moreover, it was not our intention to deny that a few deaf persons have found happiness and fulfillment in the hearing world. Persons such as the deaf Ph.D., or the extraordinary lipreader are more likely to be known by a wider audience of hearing persons, possibly unwittingly they create the impression that their situation is the norm or at least is a common occurrence. The fact is that some skills, such as really functional lipreading, are extremely rare; others, such as a good reading knowledge of English, are more common but are still nowhere near 50 percent. Finally, marriages between a deaf and a hearing partner do take place, but they are very rare and unlikely to be successful.

In addition to the few deaf adults who have adapted excellently to the hearing world and who do not belong to the deaf community, there are those who shun the deaf community but are not well adjusted socially and emotionally; psychologically they find it almost impossible to accept their condition of deafness. Finally, as was pointed out in chapter 1, some persons who are not really deaf for one reason or another choose to be part of the deaf community. Hard-of-hearing persons who can acquire language and can communicate orally, even if it is with some difficulty, do not belong here, yet at times these persons choose to join the deaf community. In this role they impersonate the proverb that among blind persons the one-eyed person is king. More frequently the choice is made for them by circumstances; perhaps as children they were sent to schools for deaf children. Children who are hard-of-hearing face a different educational hurdle from that of deaf children, but frequently one finds them in school among profoundly deaf children. Possibly a more suitable educational setting could have helped them adjust to the hearing world. However, legitimate efforts at improving the education for hard-of-hearing children need not automatically imply that a child's eventual decision to live among deaf people is psychologically unhealthy and unacceptable. For is not a hard-of-hearing person a better human being when he finds a constructive position among deaf persons than when he struggles for a marginal existence in the hearing world? Such questions must at least be seriously considered and not simply decided beforehand by a presumably absolute standard.

One other category of persons who can be said to belong to the deaf community should be considered—the hearing sons and daughters of deaf parents. These children are born into the deaf community, and their mother tongue is the sign language. They are truly bilingual and a few become eloquent spokesmen and educators for the deaf community. Further, the accomplishment of raising hearing children to be successful persons in the hearing world is another reminder that deafness need not be the isolated dark world of ignorance that one so readily assumes. The sight of a hearing child barely five years old playing the role of interpreter for his deaf parents, picking up telephone messages, and explaining to outsiders the viewpoint of deafness is one of the most remarkable manifestations of early psychological adaptation one can encounter. It reflects well on the child and his parents and beyond that on all that is good and healthy in a person in spite of, and partly because of, the challenge of profound deafness.

6

Research in Thinking Processes

This and the following two chapters summarize relevant research on deafness. The reader may have wondered why earlier chapters did not cite evidence: Why should so much controversy prevail when research could apparently provide definite results and end conflicting opinions? To answer this query we must clarify what research can and cannot accomplish in this field. But first a word about what research is.

As an illustration of research we can cite the project, to be discussed in some detail in the next chapter, on the mental health status of profoundly deaf people in New York State. Part of this project was a survey to establish a complete list of deaf persons living in the state, which required a laborious method of collecting and verifying names. In addition, statistical operations produced an estimate of the number of deaf persons to take into account possible errors such as omissions and faulty identifications. The survey revealed that about two New York State residents in one thousand are deaf:

This "researched" observation is no different from what you could do if you wanted to know if the number of girls and boys is about equal among deaf children. You could visit or write to several schools and you would soon discover that there are consistently more deaf boys than deaf girls. Some facts that research produces thus appear to be as simple as counting heads or counting boys and girls. However, frequently experts disagree even about observable facts. This uncertainty can be due to difficulties in sampling or even to such apparently trivial matters as establishing an acceptable set of identifying characteristics. For instance, who should be counted as deaf when one attempts to determine the number of profoundly deaf persons? We cite a number of surveys in the next chapter and find that each one had to choose its own, somewhat arbitrary, criterion for inclusion in the deaf sample.

More commonly, of course, disputes arise about the interpretation of facts. An interpretation is an explanation; it goes beyond the observed facts and provides a framework within which the facts make sense. Even more important, the framework often dictates which ones among the thousands of available facts one chooses to focus on. This is perhaps the factor that most dominates the direction of research—the selection of facts and the manner of their interpretation. We spoke of this general perspective in earlier chapters and shall return to it after we discuss briefly the interpretation of researched facts.

The predominance of deaf boys over deaf girls is such a fact. One could explain it by pointing to other diseases, to which the male fetus and infant seem to be more vulnerable than the female. This explanation sounds promising but is still incomplete. Why does the male have greater vulnerability to disease and why should this vulnerability affect hearing? Every interpretation or explanation invariably requires a further explanation; there almost seems to be no firm base to any scientific statement. In a sense this is correct, but for many purposes this impossible ideal of absolute certainty is unnecessary. Scientific research can accomplish much as long as one realizes its limits and does not ask what it cannot provide.

A much more serious obstacle—one related to the difficulty of establishing a generally valid set of qualifying characteristics for the observation of facts—plagues the interpretation of facts, particularly in social and educational research. We can never neatly isolate the variable in question and hold everything else constant. One cannot take two identical deaf children and educate them by the same teacher, who holds precisely the same attitudes toward each child, elicits the same interest from both, offers identical rewards and the same amount of affection to each, and devotes the same amount of time to instruction and practice with each child—in short, we cannot find two identical children and provide exactly the same environment for both—and in one case use the pure oral method and in the other a manual method of education. Realistically, all social and educational behavior is the outcome of many factors, and behavior in turn constantly affects these very factors so that it is impossible to devise a clean, neat experiment that would carry the conviction of an observed fact.

We should dwell a little longer on the difference between fact and interpretation, if only to point out how precarious the distinction is. When you read in previous chapters that the majority of deaf youngsters are failures in school, that they do not know the English language, and that they are equal to hearing youngsters in intelligence, you encountered statements that include a generous portion of interpretation. To wit, failure is not a fact but a conventional criterion of academic achievement which is arbitrary in the sense that it does not necessarily relate to the successful fashioning of human life. Knowledge of the English language appears to be a less arbitrary affair, as we tried to show in chapter 2. Nevertheless, on this point scientists do not even begin to agree, a state of affairs which can be attributed to genuine unfamiliarity with the unique linguistic situation of the deaf child. More will be said about intelligence in chapter 8, but it should be clear that intelligence, however it is observed or measured, is never a fact but always an interpretated observation by means of instruments that may or may not produce valid measures of what we call intelligence.

We must add a warning about interpreting the statistical results of the comparison of two groups, which is often the way the study of deaf versus hearing individuals is expressed. For the sake of argument we assume that all methodological procedures were meticulously safeguarded, particularly age, sex, socioeconomic status of the parental home, and physical and mental health. The performance of deaf and hearing children on a memory task is observed, a statistical average for each group is worked out, and the average of the hearing group is found to be superior to that of the deaf group. Subsequently a further statistical test is applied to find out whether this difference is big enough to warrant the following "scientific" statement: Deaf children are inferior to hearing children on this particular task. A statistical test is reasonable because averages are artificial measures that are built from individual measures that have greater or less variability around the average. But the second reason for a statistical analysis is more crucial. Our interest does not center on the particular group of children that were observed; rather, we would like to consider the group a typical sample of the larger population of all children of similar age and condition. In short, we aim at a general statement such as "Deaf children are inferior to hearing children," meaning that this characteristic would be found in other samples of deaf children. Such an observed difference is then called *statistically significant*.

What should this statement mean to you? For many people the phrase *statistically significant* turns the statement into a scientific fact, which makes further discussion out of place. If deaf children are called "significantly inferior," they are then considered general failures, whereas the investigation may merely have observed that on the average the deaf child needed six more trials to successfully recall a series of items than the hearing child, say thirty-four rather than twenty-eight trials. Does that mean that all deaf children were worse than all hearing children? Of course not. But can one at least say that 50 percent of the deaf children were lower than the worst hearing children? One can never reconstruct individual scores from averages; however, a reasonable guess would be that the upper 10 percent of the performance range included more hearing children and that the lower 10 percent included more deaf individuals. Even where there is a legitimate significant difference, it could be expected that the two groups would indistinguishably overlap across 80 percent of the performance range. In short, a *statistically significant dif-*

ference between deaf and hearing children frequently means something like this: Across 80 percent of the performance range there is no difference at all between the two groups; in the upper 10 percent there are more hearing than deaf children; and in the lower 10 percent there are more deaf than hearing children. This is a long way from statements —presumably based on statistical evidence—that deaf children fail certain tasks. Only after we grasp the meaning of these statistical terms can we interpret the results and attempt to show why they make sense.

These preliminary remarks are intended to demonstrate that a scientific fact is worthless unless it fits into a framework of a comprehensive interpretation. In the final analysis, each person must construct his own viewpoint through which to accept, modify, or reject suggested interpretations of statistical results and scientific facts. We now return to our initial question about the function of research. Research does not absolve its consumer from critical thinking. On the contrary, in the fields of psychology and education research is hard put even to supply a few unequivocal, and indisputable facts, and critical thinking is particularly necessary. Do not be awed by the phrases *critical thinking* and *scientific research*. *Research* simply means the controlled observation and intelligent interpretation of facts. This activity is not alien to ordinary human beings: in fact, no defined, invariable line separates ordinary thinking from the business of research. Everything that thinking is should be included in research and vice versa, with one obvious exception. Research, as behooves a profession, employs contrived situations and special methods of controlled observation and analysis.

The first five chapters were intended to supply an indispensable framework of thinking about our topic. They provided descriptions of deaf persons' lives, of the education of deaf children, and of the difficulty of early diagnosis and treatment of deafness. Throughout the chapters we encountered deep-seated controversies and differences of opinion. What can research contribute to these descriptive data? Can we expect research to solve the problems and controversies?

Some problems are relatively well delineated and require the specialized research of scientists. Early diagnosis of deafness, improvement of hearing aids, and prevention of deafness are areas that will no doubt directly benefit from intensive research. Other problems, such as those connected with education or low-level employment, are much more complex; they are determined by a variety of factors. Research can contribute to their better solution, but only as one contributing factor, never as the sole determining factor. In addition, the contribution is frequently indirect. Take as an example the preceding chapters in this book, which describe the life and problems of deaf people. By and large, descriptive facts such as these deal with the "typical" experience of deaf persons. But here again we face the problem of "scientific fact." For another person with a different viewpoint would have selected and presented other facets of a deaf person's life as "facts."

I want to stress that one's views of deaf people cannot be distinctly separated into those that derive from research and those that derive from direct observation of facts; research helps form one's opinion of what are noteworthy facts. A different type of research and a different type of thinking about language, knowledge, education, community, and life values would single out different facts from those presented here. As a psychological researcher in deafness, I believe that the study of deaf persons' conduct will be beneficial primarily to the understanding of the psychology of the people in general. Of course this will contribute indirectly a more adequate perspective on and a more constructive attitude toward deaf people and their problems.

If we wish to investigate the thinking processes of deaf persons, particularly children, we must use procedures that do not contain in themselves or in their instructions a strong linguistic component. Otherwise we would observe nothing but the poor linguistic knowledge of deaf children, which would be as unfair to deaf persons as judging a normal person's thinking skill by means of a verbal test conducted in a language he does not understand. Once one realizes that deaf children are not at home in the English language, one will think twice before accepting results of verbal tasks as evidence for an alleged inferiority in anything but language.

Here is a thinking task appropriate to children six to fourteen years old that was carried out entirely by nonverbal procedures (Furth 1961). The chlidren made a series of choices by pointing to one or another card. They were told each time if their choices were correct or wrong, and they were thus in a position to discover the principle that guided correct choices. On the first task this principle was symmetry, on the second it was sameness. The two cards presented to the child always included one card that showed a symmetrical drawing and one card that displayed an asymmetrical drawing. For the second task, one card always showed two drawings that were exactly alike, and the other displayed two dissimilar drawings. A third task investigated the principle of opposites. Collections of five disks of different sizes were thrown on the table, one collection at a time. The experimenter pointed to one of the disks, either the smallest or the biggest of the collection. The child was supposed to point to another disk and was corrected each time until he pointed to the opposite disk— that is, the smallest if the experimenter had pointed to the biggest disk or the biggest if the experimenter had pointed to the smallest disk. After the child discovered the principle, a subsequent transfer task studied whether he could use the principle of opposites in other situations: in length (shortest, longest), in numbers (highest, lowest), in roughness of sandpaper (least versus most rough), in color (lightest, darkest), and in spatial directions (up-down, left-right). The child indicated that he under-stood the principle in each discovery task not by verbalization of the prin-ciple but by the consistency of his correct choices.

The notion of symmetry is largely a perceptual concept that can be grasped without verbal articulation. Moreover, the proper meaning of the word *symmetrical* is unfamiliar both to young hearing children and to deaf children. The idea of *same* is based on a comparative judgment. Hearing children know and use the word *same,* and for deaf children too the sign for *same* is one of the earliest and most commonly used. *Oppo-site* is an easy conception for hearing children to understand and is deeply embedded in their language; pairs of adjectives, such as cold-hot, good-bad, strong-weak, up-down, and so on, frequently exemplify think-ing in terms of opposites to the child. Deaf children are of course un-familiar with the English words, and even the sign language uses contrast-ing terms in a much more natural, relatively continuous fashion—for example, the signs *many* and *few* are similar (in contrast to the dissimi-larity of the English words), except that the sign for *many* consists of a rapid repeated showing of all fingers, whereas for *few* two or three fingers are slowly unfolded; *big* and *small* also have the same sign, except that the hands are close together for *small* and are farther apart for *big.* Moreover, deaf children are known to have difficulty learning the ap-propriate uses of the English word *opposite.* In sum, three concepts were studied: symmetry, a notion for which neither hearing nor deaf children knew the correct verbalization; sameness, for which both groups knew a word or a sign; and opposites, for which only hearing children had a word plus constant linguistic usage.

The results of this study showed a slight improvement with age for all groups, no consistent differences between deaf and hearing children on symmetery or sameness, and consistent and fairly large differences in favor of hearing children on opposites. What do these results mean? First, that a person can understand and communicate his understanding of a logical principle without using language. Second, on the two concepts where linguistic labels were equally available or unavailable, no differ-ences emerged. But in the concept of opposites, which was purposely chosen because it creates difficulties for deaf children, they showed a re-markable lag. This lag could be described as follows: for the hearing children the opposites task was not only the easiest but it was actually too easy. Even the youngest six-year-old performed nearly without error. For the deaf children, however, it was the hardest task, and even the oldest deaf children did not perform as well as the youngest hearing children.

Before we suggest possible interpretations we should remind our-selves that the tasks on which the children were observed were ones of discovery. All we can accurately say is that deaf children were much slower or did not succeed at all in discovering the principles of opposites. This is different from saying that they cannot comprehend this principle. We have played this thinking game with young deaf children in our thinking lab, and they grasped the principle readily after minimal training.

Nevertheless, such a large difference even in discovery only should not be lightly dismissed. There are two possible explanations. Either language has given the hearing children an overall advantage in the understanding of the concept of opposites, and consequently understanding was more readily available to them in the discovery task, or this is a rare example of linguistic habits influencing thinking habits (as, for instance, in the division of hues or in phonetic distinctions, which can be different in different languages). If the first possibility were the correct explanation, one would expect to discover a broad variety of concepts on which deaf people are inferior. Such a finding would be a powerful confirmation of the ability of language to facilitate thinking. In favor of the second alternative is (1) the reported ease with which deaf children can be trained to succeed on this task (just as one can train persons to divide the color continuum differently from the way they normally divide it in their language); (2) recall that this task was intentionally chosen after observing the difficulties deaf children have with the linguistic use of the concept; (3) the almost instantaneous discovery on the part of hearing children is unusual in itself. It is reported that children sometimes play a game that is similar to the given task, and it is therefore possible that not only linguistic habits but also general play habits may have aided the hearing child.

After this study we searched for other concepts on which deaf children might demonstrate obvious inferiority to hearing children. Thus we investigated the discovery of other principles: whole-part, reversal switch (that is, an attribute that was irrelevant on task 1—for example, color—becomes relevant on task 2, and shape, which was relevant on task 1, becomes irrelevant on task 2), double alternation (a fixed sequence of correct location—for example, left, left, right, right, left, left, and so on), similarities, complex classifying, and so forth. Neither our studies nor the majority of other nonverbal studies (Oléron 1957) reported in the literature indicated any consistent inferiority of deaf compared to hearing children. As the evidence accumulated it became obvious that the first interpretation of the failure on opposites was untenable and that the second made more sense. A convenient place to look up summary evidence of past research are two reviews on deafness in the *Psychological Bulletin*—(Furth, 1964, 1971).

If deaf children's thinking is not generally inferior to or different from that of hearing children, thinking is obviously not based on linguistic ability. Otherwise deaf children who are severely deficient in knowing language should fail to a proportionate extent on thinking tasks, as they did on opposites. But, as indicated, research so far has not discovered any other concept where a similarly large difference was obtained. On the contrary, most studies show no differences between deaf and hearing children of comparable age. Studies that do report an overall retardation should be considered in the light of our discussion about the meaning of significant differences. It does not seem reasonable to attribute a slight "statistical" retardation to a general "real" deficiency in language: the majority of deaf youngsters do as well as the majority of hearing youngsters, who have language. In other words, language cannot be directly responsible for failure and success on that particular operation.

The next study shows that we can readily explain such differences without invoking linguistic factors. Two conclusions stand out in the study (Furth and Youniss 1965) to be reported: first, the difference between discovering a concept and comprehending or using it adequately; second, the effect of an intellectually impoverished upbringing on performance in thinking tasks. Both conclusions apply to studies with deaf children. Discovery is not an accurate indicator of a person's intellectual grasp of a concept. To discover by trial and error a very simple concept, such as "the second letter of the tenth word with three letters on each page of a book" could be an almost impossible task for any adult, even though its comprehension is well within the capacity of a seven-year-old child.

This particular study deals with the logical concepts of affirmation, negation, conjunction, disjunction, and their symbolization. It documents that in contrast to hearing children deaf children did extremely poorly in discovering the logical meaning of the symbols by means of a corrected matching procedure—that is, matching a written symbolic expression (for example, T/C = the disjunction of triangle or circle, excluding their combination) against a drawing (for example, a square and a circle = correct, a triangle and a circle = incorrect, a triangle = correct, a square = incorrect). Deaf adolescents sixteen years old were far behind ten-year-old hearing youngsters on *symbol discovery*.

This symbol task was subsequently modified into a task of comprehension. The meaning of the basic symbols was first clearly demonstrated, and comprehension was tested by presenting a complex set of potentially confusing instances—for example, a person had to match instances to symbols representing in turn the concepts *denial of conjunction, conjunction of two negations,* and *denial of exclusive disjunction.* (We hardly need to point out that the transmission of instructions is always a problem when one works with deaf persons and cannot rely on verbal language.) On this task of *symbol use* the same adolescents who had failed on symbol discovery performed similarly to a group of hearing young adults. This result therefore demonstrates that deaf persons, even if they have a poor knowledge of language, have and can use basic mechanisms of logical thinking as well as the average hearing person once the task is made clear to them.

Both tasks, symbol discovery and symbol use, were then administered to hearing adolescents from a rural environment in order to investigate the possible influence of a poor intellectual environment. This sample performed almost identically to the deaf sample: they failed miserably on symbol discovery and performed comparably to average persons on symbol use. The findings confirmed dramatically a hypothesis that until then was based more on theoretical than on empirical reasons: If deaf persons perform poorly on thinking tasks, their lack of a challenging upbringing, particularly during the school years, is a reasonable explanation, and lack of language is not a directly contributing factor. The rural youngsters certainly knew English and thus differed radically from the deaf adolescents, who did not know English, yet their performances with logical concepts were almost identical.

I would not deny that the "experiential deficiency" of deaf youngsters is related indirectly to their inability to hear and use language. But I blame the environment and the schools for not being sufficiently inventive to work around the language problem and to create an intellectually challenging atmosphere, just as I blame the schooling of rural youngsters for not breaking the life style of real and intellectual poverty. For Piaget, contrary to widespread opinion, language is not the preferred, much less the necessary, medium of thinking, particularly during the first ten years of intellectual development, and the deaf child is living proof of the accuracy of this statement.

In chapters 3 and 5 we briefly sketched Piaget's theory of intellectual development. We used his theory to explain the fact that a deaf person, even when he is quite poor in the knowledge of society's language, can have a sound intellect in his everyday activities. We now find that a theory of development based primarily or to an important extent on language would be hard put to explain the results of experimental research. To help you grasp the action base, as opposed to a language-base, of the mechanisms of intelligence and to complete the outline of Piaget's theory, we shall turn to two or three more studies with deaf children in the stage of concrete operations and then discuss formal operations in deaf adolescents and adults.

Another, equally important, reason for presenting these investigations of thinking processes is to make you aware of the great variety of tasks that are available to challenge and exercise a child who does not master a discursive language. In fact, it was through experimental studies of this kind that the idea of a school for thinking first arose. In the beginning the school was proposed in connection with deaf children's education only, but soon it became apparent that education of children of all types, including what we call normal children, suffers from a dearth of thinking activities. All the studies reported in this chapter lend themselves admirably to group activities which would provide children with challenging opportunities for active thinking. (These possibilities are discussed more fully in the last chapter and in Appendix 1.)

One study (Ross 1966) concerns an understanding of odds and probability judgments. The experimental setup was simple and perfectly comprehensible even when no words were exchanged. The experimenter showed the child a number of identical blocks, some blue and some yellow. Then the experimenter put a certain number of blocks into a large glass container while the child watched. For example, six blue and two yellow blocks were put into the container. The child was shown how to shake the glass so that the blocks arranged themselves in random order. A cover was then put over the glass and the child was motioned to take out one block. But before he lifted the block out of the glass, he was presented with a small board on which were fixed a blue block and a yellow block. The child had to point to one of these blocks to indicate the color of the block that he was about to draw from the glass. The child continued making guesses and then drawing the next block and looking at the actual outcome until the container was emptied of all blocks.

This probability task challenges the following thinking processes: (1) the child encounters the principle of greater, lesser, and even odds and has to make his predictions accordingly; (2) any probability judgment that is less than sure implies the possibility that the actual outcome is contrary to the more reasonable judgment; and (3) as the blocks are drawn the odds constantly change, and the child must keep track of this change. In this study deaf and hearing youngsters of ages eleven, thirteen, and fifteen were evaluated on their probability performance, first according to differing odds. Table 6.1 summarizes the results in terms of mean percentage correct predictions for hearing and deaf groups at the three age levels. Note that a score of 50 percent represents a base line of chance performance that is not guided by any rational principle.

Table 6.1 shows that the children were quite sensitive to differences in odds, so that shorter odds produced a greater proportion of unreasonable guesses than longer odds. There was consistent but slight improvement with age; however, even the fifteen-year-olds made a surprisingly large number of errors on short odds. In general boys did better than girls, and this difference was sufficiently marked at age thirteen to warrant separate entries for the sexes. Young children frequently follow a strategy of alternating predictions—that is, after guessing blue, regardless of the observed outcome and of objective odds, they tend to say yellow. This tendency was observed in our sample and predictably decreased with age; it was calculated as a mean percentage of inappropriate alternations

Table 6.1   Mean Percentage of Correct Probability Predictions of Hearing and Deaf Children, Ages 11–15, for Differing Odds

Odds	Group	Age 11	Age 13		Age 15
			Boys	Girls	
3–0, 2–0, 1–0	Hearing	83.9	89.5		92.2
	Deaf	74.7	89.0		92.7
5–3, 3–2, 4–3	Hearing	58.0	67.9	60.2	65.5
	Deaf	50.0	66.7	56.0	69.3
4–2, 2–1	Hearing	60.8	72.8	62.5	78.3
	Deaf	60.7	66.3	57.3	80.3
3–1, 5–2	Hearing	75.0	89.5	76.0	90.4
	Deaf	61.5	73.3	59.4	76.1
5–1, 4–1	Hearing	80.0	100.0	100.0	100.0
	Deaf	71.4	100.0	71.4	85.7

in two consecutive trials. At ages eleven, thirteen, and fifteen the error scores for the hearing youngsters were 51, 34, and 28 percent and for deaf youngsters were 63, 38, and 29 percent respectively.

It should be apparent that the performance of deaf and hearing youngsters is strikingly similar, a similarity that goes far beyond a global statement of no overall differences. Actually, some slight differences favor hearing children at the younger ages, but certainly the most re-markable fact is the equality of probability behavior of the sexes and on differing odds and the alternation tendencies in two groups with radically different linguistic experiences. How should we explain the acquisition of probability concepts? Does a person learn them in school or does the language of society transmit them through casual conversation? The present results offer contrary evidence to both alternatives. The deaf youngsters certainly did not learn probability as a school subject, but it is not taught to the average hearing child either. And the deaf children certainly did not learn it through informal verbal instruction from society because they cannot hear and do not know the requisite language. Nor does it make sense to attribute the relative "catching up" of the deaf fifteen-year-olds to linguistic improvement, for we know that linguistic proficiency is at a very low level for deaf persons even at fifteen years of age. In short, we need the kind of explanation of the origin of thinking capacities that Piaget provides. As the author of this investigation suggests, exposure to and active commerce with real-life probability situations affords the necessary and sufficient opportunity for the attainment of thinking competence in this area. These opportunities are open to the deaf child; knowledge or lack of knowledge of linguistic symbols is apparently largely irrelevant for the intelligent understanding of probability.

Probability knowledge is thus not a piece of information that can be taught as one teaches the name of a capital or the date of Washington's birthday. Of these latter things the deaf child is frequently woefully ignorant; he misses much information that the active child picks up from hearing what is said around him unless special, inventive efforts are made —and this does not usually happen, least of all in schools that focus on language. Nor can probability knowledge be likened to a definition, such as "an uncle is a brother of one's mother or one's father." Neither you nor I could readily frame an adequate verbal definition of probability. What type of knowledge does probability represent? It is similar to what Piaget calls an operation, a general framework of thinking that provides the mechanism for constructing a stable and objective world. This framework would enable the child to understand that in a situation of four blue blocks versus one yellow block blue is the intelligent prediction; but a contrary outcome of yellow would in no way weaken the child's stable and objective criterion of thinking, as it would in a younger child in whom the probability operation is not firmly established and who may then exclaim, "Oh, I was wrong." Quite the opposite; because of this operation, or rather in this operation, the child knows that an outcome of yellow is not at all unexpected, since it has a likelihood of one in five, although the likelihood of blue is higher—namely, four in five. The operation is an internal, structured activity and must be conceived as such. No symbolic or verbal component forms a necessary part of this activity, and consequently the operation should not be conceived as something similar to an internalized verbal or imaginal representation.

A second study that illustrates operations in deaf and hearing children with regard to comprehension of physical space was carried out by Robertson and Youniss (1969). This investigation aimed at observing children's developing competence to comprehend how physical things appear when they are spatially transformed. Two tasks were given: horizontality of water level and projection of shadows. As before, instructions for the tasks were given primarily by example so that the experimenter could be sure that the deaf children knew what was wanted of them. Sixteen deaf and sixteen hearing children aged eight to nine composed the younger sample, and two similar groups at ages eleven to twelve made up the older sample.

For horizontality a child was shown a square bottle in an upright position that was half filled with blue liquid. He was given a paper on which was drawn the outlines of the upright bottle. His task was to draw the liquid as he perceived it by making a line with a blue pen on the outlined bottle on his sheet. After successful completion of this drawing, the bottle was covered with a cloth and was rotated on a vertical plane about 45° to the right to position 2. The sheet also contained the outline of the bottle in this and subsequent positions, and the child's task was to draw the water level for each rotation. In position 3 the bottle was lying sideways; in position 4 it was at a 45° angle facing down; in position 5 the bottle was upside down; in position 6 the bottle was tilted 45° up to the left side; positions 7 and 8 were mirror images of positions 3 and 4.

Shadow projection started with an example of a square in a vertical position that cast a shadow which the child drew on a piece of paper. Then the square was tilted backward in three positions, the last of which was horizontal. Each time the child observed the shadow and then drew an outline of it after the shadow was made to disappear by turning off the light source. The task proper consisted of drawing the shadow of a straight rod as it was rotated from upright to horizontal in one vertical plane (positions 1 to 4) and then laterally on a horizontal plane (positions 5 to 8). The shadow of position 1 was a straight line that became shorter in positions 2 and 3. Positions 4 and 5 were identical; their shadow was simply a dot. In positions 6 to 8 the dot turned into a horizontal line that became larger with each position.

The procedure of both tasks included four phases. The first phase of eight positions described above required drawings as anticipated by the child; no correction or demonstration was offered. Then followed a demonstration phase, which used the first four items in each task. In this phase the child was shown the rotated bottle with its liquid or the shadow of the tilted rod after each anticipation and he had the opportunity to make a second drawing with the object in front of him. If he was still wrong, the experimenter pointed out the error and helped him to correct it. Phase 3 was a retest exactly like phase 1, with no demonstration or correction. Phase 4 observed whether improvement noted on the retest following the demonstration would generalize to a slightly different task: for horizontality a round bottle was used, for shadow projection a triangle replaced the rod.

Table 6.2 provides an overview of the results of the three test phases. Marked differences between groups of trials were observed on both tasks. For horizontality either an upright or a vertical position of the bottle (A) contrasted with a diagonal position (B). In shadow projection rotations along the vertical dimension (A) were separated from rotations along the horizontal dimension (B). The following comments summarize the results. For horizontality trials A were easy throughout, with an almost errorless performance for all but the younger deaf group in the anticipation phase only. The B trials were significantly more difficult than the A trials for all groups in all phases, and the younger children had more trouble than the older children. There was some improvement on the retest phase, which, however, did not generalize to the last phase. Results for shadow projection were similar to the pattern with the vertical trials, A trials being easier than B trials. Only in the anticipation phase were differences due to deafness observed, and this difference was limited to the younger sample and disappeared at subsequent phases. Performance

Table 6.2   Total Number of Correct Responses of Hearing and Deaf Children on Two Anticipatory Visualization Tasks[1]

Task	Age	Test		Retest		Generalization	
		4 A Trials[2] Hearing–Deaf	4 B Trials[3] Hearing–Deaf	4 A Trials[2] Hearing–Deaf	4 B Trials[3] Hearing–Deaf	4 A Trials[2] Hearing–Deaf	4 B Trials[3] Hearing–Deaf
Horizon-	8–9	63 49	26 16	63 56	35 39	63 56	17 22
tality	11–12	64 61	47 40	64 64	54 55	64 64	46 36
Shadow	8–9	58 45	43 27	62 54	42 43	22 20	18 18
Projection	11–12	59 53	54 45	61 57	54 50	29 29	39 30

[1] Maximum total per entry = 64.
[2] Horizontal and vertical positions (1, 3, 5, 7) on horizontality, vertical positions (1–4) on shadow projection.
[3] Diagonal positions (2, 4, 6, 8) on horizontality, horizontal positions (5–8) on shadow projection.

on the retest showed hardly any improvement except for the younger deaf children, and success on generalization fell sharply for all groups, young and old, hearing and deaf. Slight age differences in favor of the older children were limited to B trials.

In sum, we again note striking similarities between deaf and hearing children—similarly differential responses to trials A and B on both tasks, similar improvement with age, similar relative failure on the generalization phase. The younger but not the older deaf children were significantly inferior to hearing children, but only on the first phase. This would indicate at most a slight retardation that a short demonstration could remedy.

Thus we conclude that a lack of linguistic experience has no substantial impact on a child's understanding of spatial transformation. Contrary to traditional opinions, Piaget holds that a child's mental image of spatial relations is primarily a function of his comprehension of these relations and not simply the copying and memorizing of external configurations. This comprehension is another example of an operation, a stable framework of thinking for the coordinating of spatial movements and directions. We should conceive of this thinking mechanism not as a verbal or imaginal representation but rather as something that makes an adequate imaginal representation possible. As with probability and other systems of operations, spatial understanding is attained through active personal exposure to and handling of spatial situations. There is no necessary reason why a deaf child should be handicapped in the development of what Piaget calls concrete operations, which form a general system of thinking mechanisms directed toward the concrete physical or imaginable world. Experimental results confirm this theoretical expectation, as demonstrated above.

Before we discuss formal operations in deaf persons I would like to report briefly on the performance of deaf children on what is perhaps the best known of Piaget's tasks—conservation of a quantity of liquid

The child is asked to fill two similar beakers with an equal amount of a colored liquid, say, fruit juice. The experimenter takes one beaker, the child takes the other, and the experimenter asks the child the standard question, "Do we both have the same amount of juice to drink or do I have more or do I have less than you?" When the child agrees that both have the same amount, the experimenter takes a narrow beaker and pours his juice into it while the child watches. Because the liquid reaches much higher in this new beaker the young child's response to the standard question is likely to be, "No, you have more. It is higher." Yet when the experimenter pours the liquid back into the original beaker the child will maintain that it is the same. Or if the experimenter pours the liquid into a wide, low beaker the child may say, "Now you have less," but he again asserts equality when the liquid is poured back into the original beaker.

Piaget has found that most children between ages six and eight develop the requisite operations of quantity as the framework for comprehending that quantity remains constant throughout perceptual transformations of the material. The operations compensate for the perceived increase in height by coordinating this increase with the decrease in width. In this way the concept remains stable, or "conserved." Success on this task is considered a good indication that a child has attained a concrete operation.

As you read this procedure you may not have realized that it is almost impossible to give this task to deaf children; they simply cannot understand the standard question. Whether one uses signs or English, questions like "Which one has more?" or "Do we both have the same?" which are readily understood linguistically—but not conceptually—by any four-year-old, are riddles to these linguistically deficient youngsters. This was brought home forcefully to me when in a pretraining session many deaf children pointed to the small pile of beans rather than to the large heap in response to the signed and written question "Which one is or has more?" These children use the sign *more* when they want more to eat, and thus they understandably believed that the smaller heap needed more.

This four-word sequence illustrates why mastery of English is so difficult for the deaf person. He may be familiar with each word in a different context—for example, "*Which* color?," "*One,* two," He *has* a blue shirt," "I want *more*"—but how can one teach formally the meaning of the italicized words in this particular sequence without using language that is difficult for a fifteen-year-old hearing youngster? To sign this sequence makes just as little sense. Such a question is never used in the everyday life of children, hence their sign language repertory does not contain it, although of course it can be signed among deaf adults.

Because of this linguistic difficulty Oléron (1961) used pictorial representations for *more,* and he reported that even above age sixteen not more than 50 percent of deaf children succeeded in conversation. Furth (1966) attempted a pretraining procedure (as indicated above) to no avail for deaf children below age ten, but there was 45 percent success at ages twelve to fourteen and almost 100 percent success at ages sixteen and above. For ages twelve to fourteen Oléron reported only 20 percent success. Because these results are so different from data for hearing youngsters, one can only conclude that most of the deaf children who failed still did not understand the instructions. Thus we recently attempted another modification to adapt the task for deaf children. First, we pretended that two dolls were thirsty and wanted to drink out of the beakers. Second, we took three cardboard strips and wrote same-same on one, more-less on the second, and less-more on the third. The child was required to place one card between the dolls; the appropriate choice of the card and its placement between the dolls indicated the child's reply to the standard question. In other words, this procedure forced the child to compare the liquids with each other and to call both liquids the same or one more and the other less. We also used signs to communicate the instructions to the child. With this new procedure 67 percent of eleven-year-old deaf children and 25 percent of children eight to ten years old showed that they understood conservation.

In summary, on the same task of conservation of a quantity of liquid for deaf children below age eleven, Oléron and Herren (1961) and Furth (1966) reported zero success, although a recent modification resulted in 25 percent success. This same modification produced 67 percent success in eleven-year-old deaf children, whereas previously Furth reported 45 percent and Oléron only 20 percent success for twelve-to-fourteen-year-old deaf children.

Which of these three studies of quantity conservation appears the most meaningful? Undoubtedly the last one. The results make the most sense—a slight lag of one or two years, not the suggested five to ten year's retardation of the other studies—and there is justification for believing that in the earlier studies the requisite instructions just did not get through to the child. This then is a good example of the need for an overall perspective and a critical evaluation of research data. An additional reason why the last results appear more adequate is that a success rate of 65 percent for eleven-year-old deaf children is in agreement with results reported on conservation of quantity in Furth (1966, p. 124) for a rural group of hearing children. Consequently, on this task, as on the previously summarized task of symbol discovery, deaf children without linguistic skills performed similarly to intellectually impoverished children who had linguistic mastery. This task had some aspects of concept discovery because the procedure could not include the usual Piagetian clinical interview through which the child's thinking is explored. Finally, reports of failure are bound to be less clear-cut than reports of success.

A person's failure on a problem may be due to a multitude of causes and need not be necessarily attributed to his lack of intellectual understanding, but success on a task always manifests a positive capability that must be explained.

Everything that has been said in connection with conservation of liquid quantity is relevant to the attempt to relate formal operations to linguistic deficiency. Piaget characterizes formal thinking as operations upon operations, a thinking within the framework of the possible, the theoretical, the hypothetical. It is a combinatorial and hypothetical thinking that simultaneously takes into account different perspectives. In this aspect it differs from concrete operations, which focus on the physical and the real. The focus of formal operations is the theoretically possible, which can only be articulated in verbal or other artificial symbols. Consequently, formal thinking is often called propositional thinking. (A proposition is not a physical object but a symbolic statement of an operation.)

Most books are full of propositions, this one perhaps even more than most, as when we evaluated the results on conservation of a liquid quantity. To comprehend the arguments the reader must not only understand the language of the material but be able to assimilate the verbal material to the framework of his formal operations. This activity exemplifies mature thinking. Could a linguistically deficient deaf person comprehend the same argument? If one means could he understand the language, the answer is clearly no. But this does not tell us whether or not he would be capable of formal thinking if the message could be delivered.

In our Center for Research in Thinking and Language we approached this problem by devising thinking tasks (Furth and Youniss 1969, 1971) which seemed to be based on formal thinking but which did not require verbal instructions. Two tasks that were particularly suitable for the purpose were symbol logic and permutations. Space does not permit us to illustrate the logical symbols on which we trained deaf adolescents. This was quite different from a discovery task. We gave the young people all the help they needed, showed them examples, and corrected their errors. But why not? When you learn calculus, you receive all the help and corrections you need, yet this does not downgrade the fact that comprehension of calculus manifests your formal operations. Remember what was said about the comprehension of probability, spatial coordinations, and other operations: they are not acquired simply by external instruction and imitation but are constructed by the thinking child as he interacts with the total environment. Hence if one can "teach" any of these general concepts within a short time span, it means that these concepts were already well on the way toward being established in the child before instruction began.

Thus on symbol logic we show the adolescent that $\overline{H} \cdot \overline{B}$ signifies "absence of house and also absence of blue," whereas $H \cdot \overline{B}$ signifies "denial of the presence of blue house." Furthermore, $\bar{H} \vee \bar{B}$ signifies "either the absence of house or the absence of blue or the absence of both," whereas $H \bar{\vee} B$ signifies "the denial of either a house or blue or both." These instructions are not given verbally, but by matching pictures of real things to these symbolic expressions. Thus the child may be shown a picture of a blue tree and would have to judge that it does not match (= is not a correct instance of) $\bar{H} \cdot \bar{B}$ or $H \bar{\vee} B$, but that it does match (= is a correct instance of) $H \bar{} B$ (it is not a blue house) or $\bar{H} \vee \bar{B}$ (the absence of house is satisfied). If a person can be trained to comprehend these logical relations within two to four weeks and shows his comprehension by correctly matching symbols and pictures in many different combinations, is one justified in concluding that formal thinking has been demonstrated?

We think so and have now repeatedly shown that some deaf adolescents can succeed at this level of symbol logic and still have very poor linguistic skills. Recently we studied ten selected deaf adolescents of ages fifteen and above, all of whom had a linguistic reading level below grade 4, and we succeeded in training six of them to an almost errorless performance on this logic. Two of these were quite poor in their knowledge of English—after more than ten years in school they were still at a reading level of grade 2. In any case, six of these youngsters, who would not be able to comprehend the *language* of one sentence in this book, would comprehend very well the *meaning*—that is, the thinking operations —underlying the preceding paragraph. To investigate the stability of this achievement the six deaf students were seen again a year later and presented with a modified version of the logic task. (Instead of form and color, e.g., house and blue, two forms were used, e.g., house and tree.) After only an hour's demonstration to refresh their memory, four of these six students performed exceedingly well while the two other students succeeded on the conjunctive problems but failed on the disjunctive problems.

Another task is permutation. We provide the person with many little squares that have printed on them the numbers 1 to 6. First we take only the ones and the twos and put the pair 12 in front of him. We urge him then to continue making more pairs ("two"), but "different" pairs, until the four possible pairs, 12, 21, 22, and 11, have been completed. Now we add the threes and motion him to make all possible pairs. One of the boys in the study forms the pairs 12, 23, and 31. At this point the experimenter removes the pairs the boy had made and requires him to continue searching for new pairs. The pairs are removed to encourage him to adopt a systematic method of thinking which will make it possible to avoid duplication and to form all possible permutations without looking at the pairs. The boy continues with 13, 12, and 31 (the experimenter points out that the last two pairs are undesirable duplications); then he puts down 21 and 11. He indicates that he has finished. The experimenter urges him to find more, and the boy adds 32. After more urging he finally adds 22 and 33. The experimenter removes all pairs and writes down "How many?" The boy mentally counts and comes up with the correct answer, nine.

Now the fours are added. Before the start the boy is asked, "How many?" He guesses fifteen. Then he proceeds to form 12, 13, 14, 23, and 24; he switches the method and adds 21, 31, and 41; he hesitates, then adds 22, 33, 44, and 11, another switch that takes care of the doubles; he hesitates again (remember that all his pairs are removed from sight) and makes a third switch in method and forms 34 and 24; he is told that he produced 24 before, so he switches for the fourth time and forms 42. He is at his wit's end and from this point on he guesses and obviously makes an effort to memorize: 32, 43. He indicates that he is finished. He is asked again, "How many?" He writes down sixteen and signs, "I remember."

What can one say so far about his grasp of combinations? He is obviously working toward a system, but he does not know a fully adequate method. He is intent; for the previous answer sixteen he kept apparently all sixteen permutations in mind. We now give him the fives and ask, "How many?" His answer is twenty-four. Then he starts quickly with 11, 12, 13, 14, and 15 (observe the system; the doublet is now integrated). Now he switches and forms 21, 31, 41, and 51. He begins a new system: 22, 23, 24, and 25; followed by another new method: 32, 33, 34, 35, 42, 43, 44, 45, 52, 53, 54, 55. Finished. He is asked again, "How many?" and he replies wrongly, as at the beginning, "Twenty-four."

One can see that his combination performance is improving. He is now much surer of himself and obviously follows an internal system—there was only one major switch in his system. Now the sixes are added. The boy works so quickly that we hand him pencil and paper and have him keep the protocol. He quickly writes 11, 12, 13, 14, 15, 16, 21, 22, 23, 24, 25, 26. We stop him there and ask, "How many when all are finished?" He replies, "thirty-six?" We ask him, "Sure? How do you know?" Instead of an answer he counts the pairs he has above so far, thus indicating that if finished one could count thirty-six.

Now we hand him a lot of chips of four colors, red (R), yellow (Y), blue (B), and green (G). We ask, "How many?" He replies, "sixteen" and proceeds: RY, RB, RG; he hesitates, then forms RG. This is a duplicate; he should have put RR, but doublets often cause trouble. He continues: YR, BR, GB, YB, YG, BB, BG, GG, RR, YY. The color pairs are left in front of the boy. We notice that his system of pairing all but collapsed, but now he spontaneously forms one row of color chips from pairs starting with R and a second row underneath from pairs starting with Y. At this moment he notices the sequential order and matches the second color of row 2 with the second color of row 1; in other words, he is producing a perfect matrix. Here the experiment stopped because it was clear that the deaf adolescent had manifested a sufficient grasp of at least the elementary principles of combination and permutation.

We ask as before: How did the youngster attain the concept of combinations? Did he acquire it during the few minutes that he worked on the initial problems? In a sense we could observe how he worked his way toward a more adequate system. We could almost observe the construction of the combinatory system. However, a more accurate description is that this boy had the combinatory operation as part of his intellectual equipment before he entered the experimental situation. This task merely gave him the opportunity to articulate it fully.

Here then was a deaf boy who was very poor in the English language and not very competent or fluent in sign language, but his performance on symbol logic and permutations attested to the fact that he had formal operations. This observation alone, even if it was but one case, seems to be of far-reaching significance; it shows that not even formal operations are necessarily linked to verbal language. In fact, this is not a rare exception; we have observed about twenty-five adolescents like this over the past two years. On the other hand, perhaps an equal number of deaf adolescents were trained but offered no satisfactory evidence for formal thinking.

We believe that in this respect deaf people are similar to people from an impoverished social and intellectual environment. If the culture and the surrounding life habits do not habitually foster or at least encourage habits of thinking, formal thinking is less likely to emerge, or at least it emerges with much less frequency than in an environment that provides opportunities for thinking. On the other hand, failure to master a verbal language does not bar a deaf person from attaining a mature level of thinking if he is so motivated. This statement is not merely theoretical speculation; it follows from the evidence that this chapter has outlined.

7

Research in Personality and Social Aspects

Personality is a concept that is even more difficult to define and scrutinize than the concept of intelligence. It embraces more than intelligence does, and to this extent it is less open to scientific observation. Not surprisingly therefore, our stereotypes adhere primarily to what we assume to be the personality of the person. Disabled persons have always been subject to much stereotypic thinking. The deep-seated tendency to consider the "us" as good and normal and the "different one" as inferior and abnormal does not easily yield to a more rational attitude. Unfortunately science can be as much hindrance as help in this quest for rationality, but it is the best means available. In this chapter we consider what research can tell us about the "deaf personality," or better, because it does not assume that there is a deaf personality, we consider whether research demonstrates reasonable evidence for the existence of something typical and peculiar to the personality of deaf people.

What is meant by *personality?* Admittedly it is a vague term at best, a term that covers such diverse aspects of human life as a person's emotions and the way they are handled; moral values as expressed in his vital choices; the capacity for relating to other human beings, including cooperation within different social groups; and affection and love relations toward persons close to oneself by ties of family or friendship. None of these aspects is easily observed, measured, or compared. There is no standardized test or experimental task that will produce results having the characteristics of what one usually calls a scientific fact.

Most personality theories were developed to explain behavior disorders—the severe forms of psychosis, the more moderate and more frequent forms of neurosis, and other types of behavior disorders, including maladaptive behavior at work, in the family, in school, or in society. Leading personality theories are primarily, if not exclusively, based on clinical data—that is, they find their most adequate applicability in the field of maladaptive conduct. Normal personality development has of course been the focus of many psychological and sociological investigations, but these observations have not found a cohesive framework that would make them validly applicable to the great variety of persons living in different and constantly changing circumstances.

It is particularly difficult to isolate true personality characteristics from the cultural and societal matrix in which they develop and manifest themselves. A good illustration is tact. In general, tact is such a superficial trait that personality theories or tests do not concern themselves with it. Yet in terms of first impressions it is one of the most important social accomplishments. Tact is almost entirely a smooth conformity to social conventions that carries with it no deep commitment or personal obligation. Its positive function is obvious—namely, to avoid hurting the feelings of others unnecessarily. Its norms are largely arbitrary and moreover are in constant flux. The only way to know about them is to observe them or to be informed of them. In this respect deaf persons are clearly at a disadvantage, and thus one hears stories of a deaf person conducting himself in a manner that is uniquely silly and tactless. Such an incident has as little to do with personality as the writing of a strikingly ungrammatical English sentence by this same deaf person. Both instances mainly reveal that information readily transmitted to hearing persons did not get through to the deaf person.

Unfortunately, such events—which in themselves have nothing to do with personality traits—feed the stereotypic notion of the deaf person's lack of sensitivity. Not only are they invalid as scientific data but no general evidence of tactlessness has ever been reported; on the contrary, available surveys, summarized below, indicate the opposite. For instance, the Frederick survey questioned retail merchants about deaf people as shoppers, and the merchants' general impression was quite favorable. They even thought of deaf customers as somewhat more friendly and easier to please than hearing customers.

In other instances one neglects to take into account the relativity of personality traits. If one is an hour late for an appointment and has no adequate excuse, he is considered rude, hostile, and irresponsible in many circles of our culture. In other cultures to be late is not a big affair; rather it is expected. Similarly, in our culture any sign of bodily aggression among adults is taken as a serious lack of restraint, whereas a great deal of verbal aggression is acceptable. In other places a contrary pattern of showing hostility might be customary. Consider a deaf adult in our hearing society. Because the verbal medium is not readily available to him he may engage in behavior that for a hearing person would be a definite indication of emotional immaturity or lack of impulse control. One should not jump to the conclusion that this deaf adult has the same degree of immaturity as would be indicated by similar behavior in a hearing adult. To attack a person physically can be taken as a symptom of a negative personality trait only in relation to the total psychological situation of the individual.

This example of impulsivity is again not typical of the ordinary deaf adult. On the contrary, surveys in New York State, in Baltimore, and in the Washington, D. C., metropolitan area demonstrate that on the whole deaf persons have an enviable record, with a low crime rate and few driving violations (Schein, 1968). However, under the stress of unusual circumstances or of mental breakdown, impulsive and overtly aggressive behavior may be a more typical reaction in deaf persons than other forms of regressive behavior found in the hearing population. We can summarize this state of affairs in clinical language by stating that certain defense mechanisms that are widely available to hearing persons and that are perhaps mainly derived from internalized verbal language may not be available to deaf people. But two points must be added. First, deaf persons no doubt have some special defense mechanisms that allow them to withstand objective pressures (for example, school failure, the difficulty of communication) which would cause severe behavioral and emotional disorders in the average hearing person. (More will be said on this point later.) Second, a point clinicians are apt to forget is that persons with a wide variety of personality traits can make use of identical regressive behavior patterns in times of stress, insofar as mental disorders restrict the normal variety of the behavioral repertory. It is therefore inadmissible to infer stereotypic traits for the normal personality simply because of the relatively restricted traits of observed defense mechanisms.

The example of impulsivity is of sufficient relevance in the appraisal of deaf persons to consider it further from a developmental perspective. The five-year-old deaf child, who lives in a world in which he cannot communicate or express his feelings through the verbal medium, is bound to express his opposition, anger, and hostility through his conduct. The hearing child is able to use the verbal medium as one way of expressing hostile feelings, although this is not the exclusive or even primary medium. Nevertheless, the hearing child soon learns to use language to assert himself against peers and adults, and society uses language to inform the hearing child of reasons, examples, and rewards that mitigate the hostile-aggressive feelings of the child. On both counts the deaf child is at a disadvantage. He understands less of the world and its working, and he has no external conventional language to express his feelings to others. As a consequence, the behavior of a deaf child may appear abnormally impulsive and uncontrolled when it is compared to the standard of the hearing child. But the sensitive observer will understand that the underlying personality trait of hostility need not be greater in the deaf than in the hearing child.

Because personality traits are not absolute but relative to the person and his surroundings, occasional temper tantrums in the hearing seven-year-old child may be valid indicators of an emotional imbalance and immaturity requiring clinical intervention. But similar behavior in a deaf child does not necessarily indicate a comparable degree of immaturity. It may well be a normal and necessary developmental lag that has absolutely no lasting differential consequence on the emotional life of the healthy deaf adult and which would be comparable to one child acquiring a language from birth, another from age five, or perhaps to one child learning to read when four years old, another when seven years old. As adults these children's knowledge of language or their reading skills can be the same. Learning and development are always primarily functions of the person, and great individual variations—quite apart from environmental variations—are known to exist. But in our quest for conformity we often neglect these variations and find it difficult to admit that the immaturity in one seven-year-old child can be maturity in another child of the same age.

Most clinicians will probably have serious reservations about the reasoning of the preceding paragraphs. First, they too have fallen prey to the idol of conformity and standard behavior. But second, and more important, they assume that the verbal medium imparts a new quality and transforms the emotional life onto a higher plane. Thus they would assume a priori that a child or adult who lacked a knowledge of language must also lack emotional sensitivity and maturity. M. Lewis (1968) has devoted a whole book to this issue. He proposes that verbal knowledge of words in the area of emotions and personality should be reciprocally related to maturity of behavior. He found hardly any confirmation for his hypothesis when he tested a number of deaf children in England, but this did not deter him from stating that "the conclusion of many observers that emotional instability and inadequate sociability adversely affects the acquisition of language, does not emerge in our data. This fact does not of course, constitute evidence in rebuttal of a hypothesis which on general grounds seems highly probable. . . . Our failure to produce evidence may be one of the shortcomings of our investigation" (p. 175).

Ponder these words. The theory decrees "guilty until proven innocent," and no proof of innocence is acceptable. Actually, no personality theory can describe the personality of the deaf person because theories were derived from and based on observation of hearing persons. The possibility of not having a language during the formative years of personality development simply did not occur to the theorists. A theory can suggest some questions to be investigated, and it should attempt to make sense of observed data and to unify them, but the ultimate answers to questions must come from observation.

An interesting question concerns the relative mental health status of deaf persons, particularly the incidence of severe mental disturbance. In a recent long-term investigation (Rainer et al. 1963) into this matter deafness was assumed to be a permanent stressful state of affairs that might have serious consequences on mental health status. The deaf child's severe restriction in communicative ability, the lack of verbal language, and the deaf adult's apparent isolation within his own social group makes this assumption appear reasonable. Add to it the fact that psychosis, like most things in life, is the product of an interaction of innate and external conditions, and one has a classic experiment to test the importance of external conditions in the causality of schizophrenia. If schizophrenia is at least partially due to an unfavorable environment, a higher incidence of schizophrenia in deaf than in hearing persons could be interpreted as due to such a stressful environment.

The New York study discovered that 1.16 percent of the total deaf population in the state were hospitalized with the diagnosis of schizophrenia, compared to a rate of .43 percent for hearing persons. It was also discovered that the discharge rate for deaf patients was considerably lower than for hearing patients. I took part in this survey and recall meeting numerous deaf patients who appeared mentally adequate, but they probably were unable to request their release or find doctors who would diagnose their improved status. Additionally, because schizophrenia and deafness may both be due to a common genetic factor, this part of the survey did not conclusively answer the original question.

A second and much more probing study was then undertaken. Schizophrenic rates for siblings are known to be considerably higher than for unrelated persons. Focusing on 138 cases of deafness and schizophrenia, the study examined all brothers and sisters of these deaf and schizophrenic persons, whether living or dead, deafness or schizophrenia. Twenty-five cases of schizophrenia were found among the 284 hearing siblings and three cases of schizophrenia among the twenty-five hearing-impaired siblings. On the basis of these data the researchers computed a schizophrenia risk rate of 11.2 percent for hearing sibs and of 14.3 percent for deaf sibs—essentially no difference. Thus deafness appears to be an insignificant factor that does not contribute differentially to schizophrenia. As a corollary, personality problems specifically associated with deafness should no longer be likened to schizophrenic processes. In general the New York study from which these data were cited provided all the evidence needed to reject the notion that early deafness and its attendant problems increases the likelihood of schizophrenia.

An additional interesting, although still tentative, observation from the clinicians on the New York project is the relative infrequency of depressive symptoms for deaf persons, both in the severe form of psychoses and the more benign forms of neurotic guilt and depressive reactions. The authors suggest a link between language and depression in that the super-ego, the factor responsible for guilty self-recrimination, is in part internalized from the language of the parents. Here is a positive discovery that fits the developmental picture of both deafness and depression. It clarifies the causality of depression and at the same time explains why deaf persons are less likely to manifest this symptom.

In an effort to understand the deaf person we turn now from severe mental disorders to a description of their "normal" life as reported by scholarly investigations. Our main source is a number of recent surveys, referred to by the city where the investigation took place: New York, Washington, D. C., Baltimore, and Frederick, Maryland. A reasonable procedure would be to look for general indexes of conduct that differentiate the daily habits of deaf persons from those of the greater hearing society of which they are a part. It seems justifiable to expect that if there is a deaf personality, it should have a cumulative effect on the daily lives of deaf persons.

The first difficulty is to clarify what is meant by deaf persons and who is to be included in a sample. (The U. S. Bureau of the Census has long since given up counting the number of deaf people because invariably the figure is hopelessly unreliable.) We already know that hearing loss is not an all-or-nothing affair and that when the hearing loss occurs has an important bearing on a person's subsequent development. Old age is frequently accompanied by a gradual worsening of hearing, so that after age sixty it is rare to find a person without some measurable hearing loss. In a previous discussion in chapter 2 we distinguished deafness from hard-of-hearing status and deafness at birth before onset of speech from adventitious deafness. Throughout this book we concentrate on persons of early profound deafness because they now constitute by far the largest portion of what is called the deaf community. However, adventitiously deaf persons, because they are thoroughly familiar with the language of society, often figure prominently in the deaf community as leaders, organizers, and spokesmen.

Even though the surveys used different criteria, there appears to be reasonable agreement among the recent surveys on an estimated six to eight profoundly deaf persons in 10,000 of the general population. This rate is subject to great local fluctuations, caused, for example, by epidemics of rubella, which affects women during pregnancy and causes deafness and other handicaps in infants. These events also are responsible for a relatively high incidence of deaf children with multiple handicaps. In sum, for the United States the number of persons this book talks about is from one to two hundred thousand.

The Baltimore survey (Furfey and Harte, 1968), undertaken in the late 1960s, interviewed in detail a random sample of 137 deaf persons. Of these, fifty-two were below age twenty—that is, they were in school or were recent graduates—and seventeen of these youngsters were diagnosed as multiply handicapped. All fifty deaf adults who were in the labor force were employed, sixteen in skilled, twenty-five in semiskilled or clerical, eight in unskilled, and one in professional occupations. This gives us a realistic employment picture of deaf persons: they are definitely on the lower side of occupational status, but on the other hand, they are employed. The reports gathered from 136 employers and foremen about the quality and reliability of deaf workers were consistently positive. Within the sample there were twenty-one marriages of deaf partners, all of which were rated as stable and well adjusted; however, they included four instances of divorce in the past. The surprisingly large number of twenty marriages between a deaf and a hearing partner was discovered. In the five cases in which the wife was deaf the marriage was stable, but among the fifteen cases in which the husband was deaf, six were definite failures and two were probable failures.

The New York survey (Rainer et al. 1963) was based on a random sample of 337 marriages, among which 77 percent were rated as excellent, 8 percent as poor, and 6 percent as divorced. What emerges from both surveys, one conducted by sociologists, the other by psychiatrists, is a remarkably high rate of marital stability and adjustment. The unusualness of the high incidence of deaf-hearing marriages in Baltimore is also highlighted by the fact that of the 113 male deaf respondents questioned in New York, only eight expressed a preference for a hearing spouse. The New York survey also investigated the occupational status of 382 deaf persons and found a somewhat higher state of employment but one still below national norms: 57 percent in skilled labor, 6 percent office workers, 3 percent owning a business, and the remaining 34 percent in unskilled labor. Fewer than 3 percent of the total employable population was unemployed. A high rate of job stability was found, with 93 percent of men holding their job for more than three years. This has its positive aspect for the employer, but the negative aspects of job stability are the deaf persons' underemployment and lack of upward mobility. To illustrate that deaf persons were dimly aware of the occupational imbalance, between 30 and 50 percent mentioned some degree of unfair treatment because of their deafness. Nevertheless, fewer than 15 percent expressed open dissatisfaction with their present job. Of considerable interest for personal adjustment were answers to the question, "How do you feel about your deafness?" Of 347 replies, 62 percent accepted deafness with a natural, matter-of-fact attitude, 30 percent expressed different degrees of disturbance, and 8 percent, mostly women, appeared to deny that deafness was of any personal concern.

In another chapter of the New York project patterns of socialization and community integration were reviewed. Interview data and clinical impression indicated an adequate level of effective personal contacts. Close to three-quarters of the persons interviewed had close friends and most reported regular socializing. A remarkable 67 percent were either present or former members of deaf clubs. The importance of association for the deaf community has been mentioned before and is attested to by all surveys. Nearly 70 percent of the New York adult sample stated that they had voted within the past three years, and 84 percent reported some degree of religious activity. Both the New York and the Baltimore surveys demonstrated that deaf persons have much less trouble with the law than hearing persons.

These data summarized in the last few paragraphs confirm the general impression that deaf persons lead normal, healthy lives; throughout the book we attempt not only to convey this notion but also to make sense of it. That the obvious and severe communication handicap resulting from deafness is not a serious obstacle to healthy development of intelligence and personality is not easily accepted for a variety of reasons, particularly because of the pivotal and often grossly exaggerated role attributed to verbal language. Science often has not helped to rectify this perspective because it so often fails to distinguish between language and the person's use of it. What counts psychologically of course is the function and not the medium; the way a person uses language can vary from highly adaptive to maladaptive.

If we propose that normal development is the rule for profoundly deaf persons, we should at least mention once more the indirect benefit they have of not being exposed to forms of verbal communication that can contribute to eventual maladjustment in the hearing child. I would speculate that deaf children derive a considerable amount of ego strength from the simple fact that they are the originators and masters of their symbolic life to a much greater extent than hearing children. This theory would partly explain why deaf children can overcome obstacles that would be practically insurmountable for comparable hearing children. A related psychological advantage of deaf people should be mentioned. Deaf persons, like hearing persons, derive great psychological satisfaction from bodily communication. They find it a medium through which they can readily express themselves, and they do not mind going over the message several times to make sure it is well understood.

Just as one cannot simply rate external conduct on a common scale of psychological maturity, one cannot evaluate environmental situations as creating similar psychological stress for deaf and hearing children. When current psychological theories regard the obstacles a deaf child has to face, they predict harmful effects on intelligence and personality, and they are correct—for the wrong child! That is, by neglecting to consider sufficiently the unique quality of the symbolic life of deaf persons, they are bound to predict lasting deleterious consequences for the adult. In contrast, our effort has been directed toward clarifying the deaf child's situation from his own perspective and to accept the fact that for him verbal language is not an indispensable requirement for development. Because we did not have the easy convenience of relying on an external medium, we had to focus on the underlying psychological process. We concluded that a deaf child will use his self-originated symbols for whatever constructive purposes a hearing child may use verbal language. Thus, we did not predict any general, critical differences in intelligence or personality traits and have not been surprised at the facts cited in this and the previous chapters.

The second major fact contributing to the mental health of deaf persons is their acceptance of deafness. When in chapter 5 we implied that the choice of identity was perhaps easier for a deaf adolescent than for a hearing adolescent, we did not intend to belittle the psychological accomplishment such an acceptance implies. Undoubtedly deaf youngsters go through a crisis of identity for which their preceding life has prepared them. The important point, as demonstrated by the surveys, is that the majority of deaf persons make this life choice in a constructive manner. Interestingly, the New York survey calls it "stoical acceptance," a not-so-subtle indication of the clinicians' original assumption that the stressful situation of deafness would preclude a normal acceptance of one's life situation.

The third positive factor is linked to this acceptance of deafness. For the typical deaf youngster acceptance invariably means an implicit commitment to the deaf community, and he thus considers himself a member of a definite social group; he knows where he belongs. It is hardly necessary to emphasize how valuable this sense of belonging is for the maintenance of a stable personality. Of course group membership can carry some negative or restrictive components. First, there is a narrowness of interest, a small-town atmosphere where everybody knows everybody else. There are few secrets among deaf persons (one cannot whisper in sign language). Second, some hostility against the hearing world can be observed. This sentiment, which should cause no surprise when one considers what many deaf children have suffered from well-meaning experts, betrays itself in an unusual spirit of independence, of a let-us-do-it-ourselves attitude that contrasts sharply with the dependent atmosphere of their formal education. These three positive points have been discussed and illustrated at length in earlier chapters. They are summarized at this point to demonstrate that research findings are in accord with the general trend of our discussion. Moreover, they should help us accept and, if need be, explain the conclusion to which this chapter is leading.

If the surveys had found nothing but well-adjusted deaf persons (apart from mental illness) this would be an idyllic, although not very human, picture. Thus, having discussed the typical member of the deaf community, we can now turn to deaf persons who are less well adjusted. The Baltimore survey found eighteen cases, or slightly more than 20 percent of the eighty-five adults in the sample, that could be classified as social isolates, thirteen of them to a moderate degree, five to a severe degree. As the survey authors point out, the severe category includes four black persons who suffered the additional handicap of racial prejudice, with all the additional burdens that it entailed. Nobody who is familiar with the incidence rate of personal and social maladjustments at all levels of the hearing society would consider this percentage excessive. It is instructive, however, to note that the characteristic of social isolation is bound to be more intimately related to maladjustment in deaf persons than in hearing persons. In this sense, when the deaf person becomes maladjusted he may well exhibit some typical behavior patterns not found in the well-adjusted deaf person.

In a similar vein, clinical impressions from psychotherapeutic sessions with deaf clients might reveal a preponderance of some psychic characteristics that one could call typical, but it would be inappropriate to generalize these characteristics to the total population. Psychiatric observations from the New York project single out two points: lack of empathy or insensitivity for other people's feelings and acting out behavior or lack of impulse control together with a relative absence of obsessive-depressive symptoms, to which allusion was made earlier in this chapter. These symptoms are by definition signs of immaturity and regression, and continued research and insight into the personality of the maladjusted deaf person should help explain better their causation. At the same time one should learn to differentiate those symptoms from the varied types of more mature behavior observed in healthy deaf individuals.

Our discussion of the personality and socialization of deaf persons has so far focused on the adult and on data based on interviews and observation of adults. We described the early development of a deaf child in earlier chapters, so that the achievement of the deaf adult could be seen in an accurate perspective. Controlled data on these early phases of deaf persons are hard to gather and even harder to interpret; to apply the same standards to deaf children as to hearing children makes no sense psychologically. At best the data tell us more about the attitudes of hearing adults than about the deaf child. For instance, when teachers and counselors in a residential school for deaf children rated 11.5 percent of the children as severely disturbed and another 19.5 percent as moderately disturbed, compared to 2.5 percent and 7.5 percent for an entire public school system, one suspects that the ratings for the deaf children encompass an emotionally unhealthy atmosphere in which parents, teachers, counselors, and the entire educational system are involved.

These data form part of a recent investigation into early patterns of development and socialization by Schlesinger and Meadow (1972), a team of social researchers in California who are fully cognizant of the potentially harmful effects of the official policy of discouraging sign language, of parents torn by the conflicting counsel of experts, and of educators who have narrow and unrealistic attitudes toward the deaf child. These facets of the ordinary deaf child's environment are fully documented in their detailed report. Hence, rather than conclude that deaf children are emotionally disturbed to a far greater extent than hearing children, I would be inclined to attribute these data to what the authors (in chapter 5) call the unusual "stresses, conflicts and stereotypes" in the milieu of deaf children. In other words, they reflect attitudes of hearing adults rather than the disturbed personalities of the deaf children.

I think that there is an unresolved problem in the authors' interpretation which should be spelled out for the critical evaluation of the reader. I find it difficult to take at face value their findings that personality disturbance occurs in young deaf children five times more frequently than in hearing children, not just because these data are contrary to what I and many other persons familiar with deaf children observe but also because the low incidence of personality disturbance in deaf adults documented in this chapter thus becomes almost incomprehensible. By what miraculous turn of events would severely distrubed deaf children become well-adjusted deaf adults? I submit that such a change is more difficult to explain psychologically than to propose, as has been done in this chapter, that despite appearances to the contrary, the young deaf child has powerful positive forces of ego strength. Consequently, even without a conventional language the young deaf child is neither intellectually nor emotionally a crippled individual, and theories of intelligence or personality that rely too heavily on the critical role of language per se are simply not adequate to explain these facts.

Schlesinger and Meadow report a particularly interesting study in which the social interactions of mothers and their children were observed according to predetermined dimensions. This experiment included forty deaf children and twenty hearing children who ranged from two and one-half to four years of age. A television camera videotaped the interactions of mother and child for half an hour in a semistructured play setting. Three observers independently rated the behavior displayed on the screen on ten behavioral dimensions for the mother and ten different dimensions for the child on a scale of 1 to 8. The results demonstrated that mothers of the deaf children differed most from mothers of hearing children in their general attitude toward structuring the child's environment; they were more controlling, more intrusive, more didactic, more rigid, and more critical. These differences should not be understood as absolute, of course. Moreover, nearly all the mothers' different ratings were highly interrelated, so that a "halo" effect may have been at work.

The children's ratings on the different dimensions were less related and in this respect are more reliable. Thus the differences observed appear particularly important from a developmental perspective. In comparison with hearing children the observers found the deaf children less joyful about being around their mothers, less happy or buoyant in general mood, less creative and imaginative in play, and less excited about their own accomplishments. They were also less compliant and more resistive to their mothers' requests. No differences were found on the behavioral dimensions of normal attentiveness to a task, curious exploration, not being too dependent on the mother, amount of general body activity, and appearing generally relaxed.

It is appropriate to relate these differences to the restrictive influence of uncertain communication. The mothers feel less secure and restrict the scope of the child's activities by greater control and structuring. The children's reactions could be characterized as less extroverted, which is another way of saying that they do not as readily communicate their inner feelings. Interestingly, in the first part of this same study the authors found that within the deaf sample communicative competence was positively related to most of the dimensions that differentiated deaf and hearing children. That is, the easier it was for the mother and the deaf child to communicate with each other, the more likely it was that the ratings of the interaction during the play session would be indistinguishable from the ratings of the interaction of mothers with hearing children. The authors refer to the devastating toll that deafness can take in the reciprocal understanding and gratification of parent-child interactions, and they pay a tribute to the resilience and stamina of the children for managing as well as they do. The whole work is a forceful and reasoned plea for putting communication ahead of the educational method of oral education, if only for the sake of the mental health of the deaf children and their parents.

There is indeed a strange contrast between the relatively unexpressive and passive deaf child during the early years in his family and in school and the deaf adult who, if anything, is active, expressive, and extroverted. To the deaf child the milieu is unrealistic in its demands, hard to communicate with and understand, and lacking in acceptance of his deafness. For the deaf adult the situation is entirely different: he comprehends and adapts to its reasonable demands in vocational and social norms, he can express himself easily to his deaf friends and adequately on the few occasions when he has to communicate with hearing persons, and he can accept his deafness. Thus the personality of a person cannot be separated from the social world in which he functions. An apparently introverted deaf child in the hearing world can become an extrovert in the deaf society, and an immature, unsuccessful schoolboy can become an adult who leads a mature, constructive life in his community.

Is there then a "deaf personality?" Our answer is definitely no. We do find stereotypic and psychologically unhealthy reactions toward deafness in our society, and the inevitable result is behavior that is restrictive and immature. Some of these results are practically a psychological necessity, a kind of self-defense on the part of the young deaf person. But there is nothing inevitable about the environment in which a deaf child grows up. The new trends in research and education hold the promise of changes that will be beneficial for both the deaf child and the hearing adults who interact with him.

Our research center undertook a study of deaf adolescents, in the course of which we investigated the personality traits of these young persons. With the help of a colleague, M. Lorr who had devised and applied personality scales for a variety of populations, we constructed a behavioral

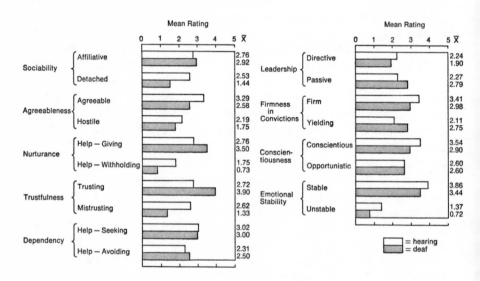

Figure 7.1.   Mean ratings on personality variables for hearing and deaf male adolescents. See Appendix 3

inventory that tapped nine dimensions of personal interactions. Each dimension had a positive and a negative pole and was represented by ten statements evenly divided between the two poles. Two observers who were well acquainted with the students were asked to concentrate on one person at a time and go over the ninety items, indicating with a plus or minus whether a specific statement was true (or more true than false) or false (or more false than true) for the particular person. This was done for twenty-seven young deaf men around age eighteen and a half. They were neither the best (being enrolled in the school's "academic" program) nor the worst in scholastic achievement but represented a typical sample of deaf persons entering adulthood.

For a control hearing group we obtained ratings on fifty hearing boys in a residential school. Their mean age was two years younger than the deaf adolescents; however, they were comparable to the deaf boys in that they were in the last grades of high school. Figure 7.1 displays the average ratings on the nine dimensions with their positive and negative poles. The following personality assessment of the "average deaf adolescent "is based on the data of figure 7.1.

In comparison with hearing norms the deaf adolescent is somewhat more sociable and is less inclined to remain aloof from others. He is generally more helpful toward his peers than are hearing boys. Moreover, he is quite a bite more trustful and open toward others. In social leadership he is somewhat below the average of hearing young men. In the important area of emotional stability he is well in control of his emotions; compared to hearing boys he is less given to worry and introspection. He is somewhat less tolerant when irritated by others, but at the same time he is in no way more hostile toward others. He appears to hold convictions less firmly and is somewhat more suggestible. He manifests a normal degree of independence and a willingness to ask for help. As for maturity in moral behavior, he is not overly selfish or opportunistic and is only a little less reliable or principled than hearing boys. In sum, the only differences that could be labeled "typical" are that young deaf men seem to have a greater degree of helpfulness and trust than young hearing men, which may reflect a measure of naiveté and closer ties with members of their in-group.

The students' records revealed that some of these boys had been difficult at home and at school and had done childish and silly things probably longer than hearing children normally do. However, the important point is that the great majority of deaf children mature rapidly as they enter adolescence and adulthood and responsibily take over their own lives. A few may not successfully make this transition, and a mental breakdown may reveal the early immature patterns of conduct. But these are exceptions, and no evidence has shown that they occur more frequently in deaf persons than in hearing persons at an adult age.

8

The Testing of Deaf Children

In this chapter we turn our attention to standardized tests of various types and their use with deaf persons. We also include a few typical studies that deal with educational procedures. Rather than singling out particular tests, we are concerned primarily with the underlying assumptions and the function of these tests, and we stress the extraordinary caution that must be exercised if they are used with a nonstandard population.

A first question that needs clarification concerns the basic idea of standardization. It is widely believed that experts are tolerably well acquainted with all kinds of normative facts. Psychologists are thought to have a ready supply of tests that can produce a measurable score for any individual on various traits and skills. However, quite the opposite is true. Language is an apt illustration. Does any solid data exist on the time of the onset of speech or on how linguistic knowledge can be measured? A healthy child of twenty-five months who does not yet speak a single word is probably still within the normal range. But one can also find a child of ten months who speaks one word. When one deals with a fifteen-month range in a one-year-old child it is obvious that standardization that would place a child at a fixed point relative to other children does not make much sense. Reference was made before to deaf children's poor knowledge of English, but how do we measure it? By reading tests, which are basically unrelated to a knowledge of language. Actually, reading tests take a knowledge of language for granted, but we use these tests on deaf children for lack of any better instrument to measure knowledge of language. This is a good example of a situation where normative facts and valid tests for knowledge of language are simply not available, although they could aid our understanding of deaf children.

Underlying the notion of many standardized tests is the concept of normal distribution. With reference to a trait or a skill that is common to all human beings, normal distribution refers first to a mean or average score. Two-thirds of all persons would cluster around this mean, one-third a little above the mean and one-third a little below; only a relatively small proportion would score farther out from the mean, again in a symmetrical fashion, so that a small fraction would score exceptionally high and a similar fraction exceptionally low. For physical and physiological measures such a concept works beautifully; height, weight, strength of pulling, reaction times to sound or light, and so on can be measured, and researchers would find the scores of adults in our society to be normally distributed.

With psychological traits and skills, however, the assumption of a normal distribution is problematical and is at best a theoretical assumption. Theorists often hold that a variety of innate factors in interaction with environmental factors—all bearing on a certain behavior—are bound to result in a normal distribution of this observable behavior, but there is no biological necessity for this conclusion. Even if we could test linguistic knowledge, could not 95 percent of the population have the same score and only 5 percent score poorer? In such a case any standardized test score would indeed be impossible. At the most we could single out the few who are below the great majority in linguistic knowledge and give all others the same positive score. Is not this what physicians do when they give children a physical checkup? They look for unusual signs or for a score that clearly falls outside an expected range on a variety of vital aspects of physical health. In most cases they give the child a clean bill of health, and the public is grateful and is willing to pay for this service.

If it is difficult to find a normal distribution of measurable scores for many facets of well-known physiological functioning, why should we expect a normal distribution on the far more complicated and less well understood level of psychological functioning? Perhaps a case could be made for postulating a normal distribution if only innate, hereditary factors were involved, but because all psychological functioning can only be conceived as at least partially dependent on environmental factors, one must examine whether the environment does indeed represent continuous random variations around a stable mean.

When we limit our view to a narrow segment of a relatively stable and homogeneous society we may be able to justify the assumption of a normal distribution for some environmental aspects. But as we widen our perspective and cross over to different subcultures within the society and to other societies, we definitely lose the assumption of a standard environment on which standardized tests are built. There is no continuous, gradual variation from a black inner-city environment to a white middle-class suburb, but rather an abrupt switch from one to the other; the situation in which a deaf child finds himself is similarly not quantitatively different—a little more or less—but in many aspects it is different in quality. For instance, the deaf child does not have a language system at his disposal, whereas the hearing child does. And because language is closely related to the communicative aspects of test performance and test instructions, the testing of deaf children obviously poses a special problem.

Before we approach this problem directly we must ask ourselves, What is the purpose of testing deaf children? What do we want to know? Perhaps the most urgent question is impossible to answer: How would the child have scored if he had not been deaf? This is the kind of question that is nearly as unanswerable as the quest for the true innate potential. One can sympathize with its motivation, but scientists must resist this temptation to determine contingencies that did not happen.

Innate potential implies that every infant is born with the potential to develop according to alternatives that are limited in a sense but that are also quite undetermined and open-ended. This is the paradox of human life, and we must be careful not to deny it by the kind of question we ask. There is no one optimal innate potential, just as there is no one fourteen-year-old hearing girl who represents what the fourteen-year-old deaf girl would have been if she had not been deaf.

I have listed the desire to measure true innate mental capacities with the chimerical search for the nondeaf double of a deaf original because both notions are equally based on an inadequate psychology of development. Yet the concept of a measurable innate potential is still commonly held in connection with so-called intelligence, or IQ, tests. It continues to provide fuel for the fruitless heredity-environment controversy and lies at the base of the distinction between general ability tests and special achievement tests. Ability tests, including intelligence and aptitude tests, are supposed to be primarily determined by hereditary factors, whereas achievement tests measure the results of special learning. However, the ideal of a "culture-free" test of intelligence is no longer seriously maintained, even by scholars who stress the importance of innate characteristics. Environmental factors too obviously influence the level of performance on any task that purports to measure intelligence.

Intelligence tests have always been closely related to academic performance—they were used initially as a selection procedure to admit children to school—and even now the single measure that correlates best with the IQ score is simply a vocabulary test. Knowledge of what a word means evidently depends on the environment in which a child grows up and, even theoretically, can hardly be related to innate factors. Moreover, in recent years numerous widely publicized efforts have been made to raise the IQ of children from disadvantaged areas. If we can raise an IQ score through appropriate instruction, it means that the basic difference between IQ tests and achievement tests has been effectively eroded. The IQ test then cannot measure the innate mental potential as if this potential were an entity impervious to environmental influences.

The implications of this discussion for the interpretation of IQ scores on deaf children should be obvious. In addition to the two reasons for testing already mentioned, deaf children are being tested simply to find out how they stand in comparison with comparable hearing children. A number of difficulties arise here, not the least of which is the problem of a meaningful control group. Also, who should be included in a deaf sample? Frequently schools or classes for deaf children have a heterogeneous mix of children—they come from different socioeconomic backgrounds, have differing degrees and onsets of deafness and differing attitudes toward deafness, and include a relatively high proportion of children who suffer from additional physical handicaps. Deafness has been called a great leveler in the sense that differences in class and life style are perhaps less extreme among deaf adults than in the hearing society. But for deaf infants, as for all children afflicted with a handicap, the opposite is usually true. There is no typical environment, no standard way to react to and manage deafness. Each child and each family must face their uncommon burden in an individual manner. As a consequence, deaf children are subject to a greater than usual variety of environmental influences, and a meaningful interpretation of a standardized test score becomes that much more difficult.

The most common setting for testing is of course the school, and the frequency of testing seems to be directly proportional to the relative failure of the student. The deaf child is probably one of the most frequently tested individuals in this country. Achievement tests are routinely administered, and most deaf children are also given some type of intelligence test. If the child is a behavioral or diagnostic problem, he will receive a variety of other tests.

Some intelligence tests are nonverbal—that is, they do not require comprehension of verbal discourse as part of their procedure. From what is known about the low level of language skill in deaf children, verbal tests are quite unsuitable. However, even with nonverbal tests the instructions are presented orally to hearing youngsters: "Show me what is missing in the picture," "Point to the one that goes with it," and so on. Young deaf children do not understand sentences of this sort, either in oral or written form. The examiner must rely on gestures and examples or on the lucky chance that the deaf child will cleverly guess the meaning of the task.

This of course is much more difficult with younger deaf children than with older ones. I recall a deaf child who was given a test of "picture completion." The child was shown a series of pictures, each of which had some conspicuous part missing. Since the particular child did not catch on immediately, the examiner pointed to the table and with his index finger counted the legs—one, two, three, four, but the fourth leg was missing. The child smiled, the examiner smiled, and the test proceeded. For each subsequent picture the child reacted as he thought the examiner wanted him to react. He put his index finger on the picture and said, "one, two, three, four" and looked up happily, expecting the smiling approval of the examiner. This might seem like senseless, perseverative behavior, but we must realize that education frequently trains and rewards the deaf child for doing exactly that—at least from the child's viewpoint. However, this example was not a case of perseveration but a case of misunderstanding. In general, the problem of instructions can be overcome; the sensitive examiner will use enough examples to make sure that the instructions have been understood.

Two other test aspects tied to verbal discourse are more subtle and less easy to control than instructions. First, there is the atmosphere of the testing situation, in which an occasional "You are doing fine" or "Well done, continue" contributes a critical share. It is not easy to find an equivalent of these unobtrusive remarks for the deaf child. A sign for "hurry up" takes the attention of the child away from the task and slows him down. It thus seems wise not to give timed tests at all, at least not to young deaf children. Similarly, a gesture of general encouragement can be taken as a sign of specific approval. The child will then naturally look for continued approval and will pay more attention to the face of the examiner than to the task. Or conversely, this same gesture may make the child uncertain. If he is not quite sure what the task is, he may interpret a general gesture of "continue" as a sign of mild disapproval and be led in the wrong direction.

Second, and related to the general atmosphere, is the problem of assuring that the child is free from test anxiety. With a hearing child, the examiner speaks a few words, involves him in active interchange, and explains the test situation as an interesting occasion. The deaf child is as anxious as all of us are in an unfamiliar situation. It takes ingenuity and time to establish rapport by letting the child play with something, because easy, informal conversation is usually out of the question. Even then the examiner cannot be sure to what degree test anxiety interferes with performance.

In a similar vein, some deaf children might be poorly motivated to attend to the task and might be happy simply because they are in the presence of an adult who pays special attention to them. We observed another example of a poor test attitude when during one of our investigations we worked with deaf youngsters on tasks of symbolic logic. When we thought they had comprehended the logical use of the symbols, we gave them a test and were surprised to find that even the best performance contained 20 percent mistakes. When we pointed this out the youngsters were in turn surprised at our displeasure. Why should we not be satisfied with 80 percent success when in their daily scholastic achievement they hardly ever reached a success rate as high as 80 percent? We then gave them a similar test and insisted that 20 percent error was not good enough, that we wanted *no* error. We then had several errorless per-formances. This experience shows what can happen when the child changes his attitude and tries to do as well as possible and is not satisfied with just being correct a few times. I have also observed on several oc-casions that a deaf child, to a considerably greater extent than is usual in the hearing child, will improve his level of performance on a paper and pencil test merely by being given a second opportunity without any correction whatsoever.

Because of these difficulties it might appear that deaf children would perform rather poorly on nonverbal tests of intelligence, but surprisingly their overall scores have never been demonstrated to be *greatly* lower than national norms, although occasionally some significant differences in favor of the hearing norms are reported. Even then, differences are usually limited to the lower age level—that is, to the age when deaf children are particularly likely to misunderstand test instructions and to feel anxious about the test situation. On an individual level, nonverbal in-telligence tests are frequently and successfully given to deaf children, and standard norms can be used; with the proper precautions and with few exceptions, the resulting IQ score appears to be as valid for deaf children as for hearing children.

These general results have been known for a long time, and they confirm the belief that what these tests deal with and what these children obviously have is a kind of intelligence that is different from the intelli-gence that deals with language. For as we mentioned before and shall document presently, these same deaf children who perform normally on nonverbal intelligence tests fail rather miserably in language learning (Vernon 1968). There is some justification in considering nonverbal intelligence tests of a lower logical order than typical verbal tests, and many people would thus conclude that deaf children may well have a normal concrete intelligence but apparently lack abstract intelligence. Moreover, those who say this imply that abstract intelligence is more or less the same as verbal intelligence.

A more adequate response to the test data would be to disregard the distinction between test types and to consider these tasks as primarily testing general achievement; this would demonstrate that the deaf child is as skilled as the average hearing child in the use of sight and in the manipulation of physical things. However, it is a mistake to consider the intelligence that deals with verbal material as different from the in-telligence that deals with visual objects. In fact, verbal intelligence can be considered more primitive than the intelligence that deals with many so-called concrete tasks, if by verbal intelligence we mean the intelligence to acquire language—hearing children know and speak this language long before they can master even the easiest form of many nonverbal tasks.

On the other hand, if by verbal intelligence we refer to logical thinking of a high order, intelligence tests may not be a good source for tapping this ability. In this respect standardized nonverbal tests are even less satisfactory than verbal tests. But experiments such as those described in chapter 6 demonstrate sufficiently that deaf persons without language can manifest a highly developed form of logical thinking. In sum, knowing that a deaf child compares favorably with a hearing child on visual and manipulatory skills is interesting; and this is primarily what nonverbal test data supply. But for the educator who focuses on the teaching of language, the results of intelligence testing are not overly helpful and are of small importance when evidence demonstrates that the deaf child certainly has adequate logical intelligence. All the teacher is left with is the fact that the child is poor in language, which he knew before administering the test.

Why then does the educator of deaf children ask for intelligence tests? This is perhaps not a fair question. Why does the teacher of *any* child ask for intelligence testing? If classroom activities were primarily designed to nourish the spontaneously developing intelligence, the teacher would not ask for special intelligence tests because all year long he would have ample opportunities to observe and evaluate the child's intelligence at work. And his observations would be more valid and enlightening than performance scores on any conceivable standardized test. If this is true for the average hearing child, it is a hundred times truer for the deaf child.

The reader is by now no doubt aware that I am less than enthusiastic about the use of standardized tests. I consider them of little scientific value, their educational function is at best questionable, and all too often they lend themselves to misuse and misguided interpretation. One would expect that similar strictures would not apply to scholastic achievement tests, since one merely tests and evaluates the supposed progress in teaching. But let us look at some facts and discuss their interpretation. In May 1959 the reading performance of deaf children was comprehensively surveyed, and the results were published as Special Deaf Norms of the Metropolitan Elementary Reading Test (Furth 1966). Based on over 5,000 pupils in schools for deaf children the mean scores on reading rose steadily for an initial 12.6 for the youngest group (ages ten and a half to eleven and a half) to 21.6 for the oldest group tested (ages fifteen and a half to sixteen and a half). If we compare these scores with the norms published for a large national sample, we notice that the mean score for the youngest group corresponds to a mean grade equivalent of 2.7 and that the score for the oldest group corresponds to an equivalent of grade 3.5.

Here in a nutshell is the problem of education for deaf children. The one educational objective to which nearly all energies are turned is language. The colossal reading failure (as summarized above) reflects a deficiency in the knowledge of language and not, as would be the case with hearing children, a reading disability. These results caused no excitement when they were published. Any large school for deaf children that does not select its pupils has lived with these facts, and surveys have never reported an appreciably different picture. A person who has been profoundly deaf from birth and who can read at grade 5 or better is invariably an exception.

One could perhaps consider a reading score of grade 4.9 or better a reasonable cutoff point between pupils who have reached a functionally useful reading ability and those who may know some English but could be characterized as functionally illiterate. Using this criterion, the reading norms would find 1 percent of deaf children at age eleven functionally literate; this figure rises to 12 percent at age sixteen. Because the survey

Table 8.1   Grade Equivalent Means Performance of Deaf Children as a Function of Age and Test Battery

Battery	7	8	9	10	11	12	13	14	15	16	17	18	19
Primary I	1.64	1.82	1.86	1.89	1.94								
Primary II				2.97	2.61	2.49	2.60	2.50					
Intermediate I						3.35	3.39	3.20	3.24	3.26			
Intermediate II							4.08	4.43	4.31	4.30	4.10		
Advanced									5.54	5.77	5.90	5.79	5.68

excluded multiply handicapped deaf children but not those who were adventitiously deaf, the percentages are probably inflated by those who became deaf after the acquisition of language.

Ten years later an even more inclusive survey of academic achievement test performance of hearing-impaired students was undertaken; close to 12,000 children were given the Stanford Achievement Test. Table 8.1 shows the mean grade equivalent performance on paragraph meaning for the severely deaf youngsters on the basis of published results (Gentile 1969). The table separates age levels from ages seven to nineteen and the different test batteries that were considered suitable for youngsters at a particular age level. For instance, some of the thirteen- and fourteen-year-old students were given Primary II, some Intermediate I, and some Intermediate II.

The entries represent mean grade equivalent scores on the paragraph meaning subtest. To discuss the results, consider first the last row, the Advanced battery, given to fifteen- to nineteen-year-olds. Scores do not go up from year to year, but stay at the mean score well above grade 5. At first glance this achievement seems to be an improvement over the findings of the earlier survey, but look at the row above, the Intermediate II battery; again there is no progress with increasing age, but a stationary level just above grade 4. A similar situation holds for the other rows. These results could be due to the fact that deaf children who did better in school were given more advanced tests. Thus the slowest fifteen-year-old youngsters were given Intermediate I, the best youngsters Advanced, and the group in between Intermediate II. This procedure was probably followed and may partly explain the progress from row to row and the curious absence of progress from left to right along each row.

Unfortunately, the given mean scores are close to meaningless because the batteries are designed to make them suitable for certain grade levels; they are thus inappropriate and unreliable for measuring performances that are well above or below the recommended grade. The Advanced battery is recommended for grades 7–9, but only about 22 percent of the more than 1,100 students who took the test represented in the last row of table 8.1 reached or bettered the equivalent of a reading score of grade 6.5, one-half year below the lower limit of the test. Intermediate batteries II and I are recommended for grades 5–6 and grades 4–5 respectively. Here too the mean scores are considerably below the lowest suggested grade. For the two Primary batteries, covering the second half of grade 1 to the end of grade 3, the mean scores stay close to the lowest possible scores.

By chance alone anyone taking the Advanced battery would score 4.8; with the Intermediate II and I tests chance scores would be 3.6 or 2.8; and with the Primary batteries scores would be 1.9 and 1.5. In other words, the mean scores of table 8.1 are not much above chance scores, and because the majority of scores pile up at the chance level, these mean scores are obviously inflated. In sum, the data of table 8.1 are primarily due to the type of battery given and cannot be considered a valid picture of the reading level of deaf youngsters. If we count the number of deaf students whose scores can be considered meaningful, we find that the results of the 1969 survey do not substantially differ from the 1959 survey. For instance, 20 percent of the 540 pupils of ages fifteen to seventeen who took the Intermediate II tests reached a reading grade of 5 or better. This 20 percent is a more realistic picture than the claim (on the basis of the last row in table 8.1) that about 50 percent of deaf students reach a grade 5 reading level.

There is no easy solution to the problem of evaluating the results of education. But given these results, at least one pertinent question should be raised: Why do schools for deaf children use tests that were meant to test the reading skill of children who know language? It is surprising that no one has constructed special tests to evaluate deaf children's knowledge of language. Instead of the meaningless assessment that is reflected in the almost stationary reading scores of table 8.1, such a language test could potentially help both the teacher and the child by focusing on the first task, which is learning to know a language; learning to read is a secondary task.

These test results also highlight another dilemma in the education of deaf children. Certainly one of the reasons national reading tests are given to children who do not even master the rudiments of the English language is public pressure and the desire for conformity. For a similar reason every year thousands and tens of thousands of hearing children in this country are tested and prove to us and, what is more harmful, prove to themselves that they are failures and apparently without the aptitudes to succeed in our competitive society. Fortunately, deaf children seem to be much more immune to scholastic failure than hearing children, and they take the routine of testing and failing with good grace.

Earlier chapters alerted us to the competing and often conflicting educational methods for the deaf child. What can scientific research contribute to the resolution of these arguments? It would be naive to think that any one experiment could solve all unsettled questions. Oralists regularly argue that one should use only oral communication and training with very young deaf children, because permitting a visual-manual type of communication would interfere with the potential success of oral education. They provide nothing but anecdotal evidence on this point, but since oral education has been dominant for so many years, the other side must show that the argument is ill-founded. Three studies undertaken in recent years intended to show that exposure to manual language at an early age does not interfere with progress in a traditional school envioronment.

Stuckless and Birch (1966) selected thirty-eight deaf children around a mean age of fourteen and a half years who had deaf parents and were thus exposed to the American Sign Language from birth. They matched these children with deaf children who were born to hearing parents and had not had early contact with sign langauge. The investigators then tested these two groups of deaf children on a variety of scholastic tests and discovered slight differences favoring the children who knew sign language on three tests—reading, written language composition, and lipreading inventory. No differences were observed on speech intelligibility or on a pupil adjustment rating scale.

Meadow (1968) performed a similar study with fifty-nine deaf children of deaf parents. She reported that these children were superior to a control group of deaf children on Stanford Achievement Grade Average, most conspicuously on reading (mean difference, 2.10 years) and arithmetic (difference, 1.25 years). On lipreading there was no difference between the groups, but on a variety of scales on social adjustment the deaf youngsters from deaf homes rated higher than the deaf children from hearing homes.

Working in a residential school, Vernon and Koh (1971) selected twenty-three deaf children of deaf parents who had a manual pre-school experience, and compared them to an equal number of deaf children of hearing parents who had the benefit of early oral preschool experience and another group of deaf children of hearing parents with no preschool training. At a mean age of eighteen years these three groups achieved the respective mean grade scores on reading average of 7.3, 6.0, and 6.0. These and other data demonstrate again that manual experience aided scholastic achievement more than oral preschool experience and that it had no negative effect on speech and lipreading; a second, potentially far-reaching, finding was that the oral preschool children performed no better than the deaf children of hearing parents who attended no preschool.

These results are of considerable help to those who advocate the early use of manual language; the manual language apparently has no harmful effects on the learning of English speech and language—if anything, the results indicate some positive advantages. However, three considerations could weaken the impact of these studies. First, from what we know about the deaf child's early years at home, deaf children of deaf parents enjoy an obvious advantage over deaf children of hearing parents because their deafness is accepted and they are given social and emotional security. This factor rather than early acquisition of sign language could be responsible for achievement superiority. This point may be valid, but it is not decisive, for if sign language can contribute to the parents' acceptance of their deaf child and thus indirectly lead to better academic progress, early signing should be recommended for this reason alone.

The second objection is more crucial. Oralists have pointed out that the control groups did not have the benefit of a *genuine* oral education. In other words, they would argue, these studies did not really test the potentially harmful effects of sign language on a strictly oral education. This may well be true, but the paradox is that strict oral schools are not cooperative when they are asked to take part in studies of this kind. As a matter of policy they do not admit to their schools a deaf child who knows sign language, since he would certainly "contaminate" the other children with his signing. Thus there is no way of conclusively testing this question—not because investigators cannot frame a scientifically acceptable research design but because social realities are more powerful than the rigorous requirements of science.

A third point turns the initial hypothesis around. Rather than speculating that early signing interferes with English speech, one expects that signing increases the likelihood of better progress in English. All three investigations support the expectation of a positive transfer, but not decisively: Stuckless and Birch, for instance, report a mean reading level of 3.9 as compared to 3.4. A reading level of 3.9 is better than 3.4, but it is still a very low score for fourteen-year-old youngsters. However, this third point is not well taken. The children who were studied attended traditional schools that did not make constructive use of the sign language in the curriculum. They were in an oral academic atmosphere. What these studies primarily show is the fact that early signing did not seriously interfere with this oral curriculum; they do not tell us what signing could have done for these children if the school had wholeheartedly and constructively accepted signing and integrated it in an overall program. The new approach of total communication aims at such an integration, with signing as the common coin of exchange. But the approach is still relatively new, and to learn its strengths or weaknesses we shall have to wait until children educated under this method grow up.

A finding from the Baltimore survey ties in with the three previous reports. The investigators in Baltimore divided their adult sample into

Table 8.2   Hearing Status and Communication Skill of Deaf Adults Who Attended Oral and Traditional Schools

School	N	Mean hearing score	Mean communication score	
			With deaf persons	With hearing persons
Oral	31	2.32	1.76	2.84
Traditional	14	1.13	3.04	2.96

those who as children attended an oral school and those who went to a school that used a combined method. Table 8.2 indicates the mean hearing level of these two groups and the mean communication score for conversation with hearing or deaf persons. The scores range from 1 to 5. The results show first that the combined-method school had a population with a more severe hearing loss, but when these children grew into adults they were much better prepared to communicate with other deaf persons than those who had less hearing loss and attended oral schools. However, the two groups were essentially the same in communication skill with hearing adults.

Such findings, although they were not as well controlled as experimental studies, are more important from a practical standpoint, for they deal with the product of education, the deaf adult. The most pervasive argument for oral education has always been that this is a hearing world and the deaf adult must adjust to it. However, oralists forget that adjustment can take many different forms and that these need not involve total neglect of the deaf community and exclusive concentration on the hearing society and its speech. But even on this score the average product of oral education is not impressive according to table 8.2. If the claim for success is invariably based on a few selected individual cases, the merits of oralism as a general, primary educational policy are indeed weak and should be subjected to scientific scrutiny.

In chapter 4 we mentioned the introduction to this country of fingerspelling at the beginning of the 1960s, which was partially in response to claims of its successful use for the education of deaf children in Russia. Quigley (1969) set himself the task of evaluating fingerspelling as an educational method. For this purpose he performed two investigations, a survey and an experimental study, the main results of which are summarized in table 8.3.

The survey sampled the scholastic performance of more than two hundred deaf youngsters over a four-year period. Half the children attended traditional schools, where there was early emphasis on oral education but later permissiveness about signing to enable the older students to communicate during the process of education. The other half of the sample attended schools that had recently introduced fingerspelling to accompany speech, which in practice meant that whatever a teacher spoke he also spelled with his fingers; the deaf child was encouraged to do likewise—to speak and fingerspell at the same time. The mean age of these children was thirteen years during the first year and seventeen years at the end of the four-year investigation.

Table 8.3 lists the battery of tests the children were given. We can see that in the first year they were well matched in achievement levels except in fingerspelling. After four years the experimental group was, as expected, still superior on fingerspelling, but they were also better on the Stanford Achievement Test, the reading test, and the battery median, as well as on a test of grammaticability. In speechreading and speech intelligibility and on two written language tests the two groups performed comparably.

The author interpreted the results cautiously because these children had been in school several years before they were exposed to regular fingerspelling and because the educational procedures in the participating schools could not be carefully controlled. Nevertheless, the increased achievement of the fingerspelling youngsters suggests that the children benefited directly from easier communication, and the similar scores on speech and speechreading indicate no harmful effects of fingerspelling in these areas.

The second experimental study was a more decisive and better controlled investigation, pitting oral education plus fingerspelling against pure oral education. Sixteen deaf youngsters around age four and a half were selected for the two educational treatments. The results four years later are summarized in the right portion of table 8.3. A fairly consistent

Table 8.3   Summary of Educational Achievement for Deaf Pupils in Programs with and without Fingerspelling

Tasks	Survey				Experimental Study	
	Year 1		Year 4		Year 4	
	Fingerspelling N = 112	Traditional N = 110	Fingerspelling N = 92	Traditional N = 91	Fingerspelling N = 16	Oral N = 16
Fingerspelling	62[a]	44	80[a]	68	34[a]	2
Speechreading						
Words	62[b]	67[a]	68	72	45	40
Sentences	58[b]	61[a]	65	63	38[a]	23
Speech Intelligibility	16	19	22	24	—	—
Stanford Achievement						
Reading	3.5	3.4	4.6[a]	4.0	2.3[a]	2.0
Battery media	3.9	3.7	5.4[a]	4.7	—	—
Written Language						
Type-token ratio	52	50	56	55	—	—
Grammaticability ratio	81	79	87[a]	83	—	—
Sentence length	7.3	7.4	8.9	8.5	5.8[a]	4.5

[a] Significant differences favoring students who knew fingerspelling.
[b] Scores for year 2.

improvement with fingerspelling as compared to oral training is evident, including even the sensitive area of lipreading.

Quigley's conclusions are open to the previously mentioned criticism that no strict oral control group was used. A more valid concern seems to be that fingerspelling should be of considerable benefit. Those who are interested in using fingerspelling or the American Sign Language as a contribution to the education of deaf children cannot be satisfied with the mere demonstration that neither has any harmful effects. What is needed is an educational setting that is psychologically sound and that eliminates the human tragedy of failure and intellectual discouragement. In this respect none of the three controlled studies are overly encouraging. Quigley appropriately remarks that his findings confirm the advantages of fingerspelling—just as Stuckless and Birch and Meadows can suggest an advantage for early signing—but the results do not mean that fingerspelling or signing is a panacea for the pressing educational problems.

This brings us back to the end of chapter 4, where the new trends in the education of deaf children were discussed. We asked whether total communication is truly a new perspective in the education of deaf children and whether the spirit of innovation would go far enough and deep enough. If total communication is primarily a way to help the young deaf child and his hearing parents and teachers become acquainted with fingerspelling and the American Sign Language, this may be a valid goal in itself, one that will no doubt have long-range beneficial effects. But will the educational achievement be substantially higher? The studies we reviewed hardly provide evidence in favor of this fond hope. After all, the children of deaf parents come to school knowing sign language. They may generally become better students than those who do not know the sign language, but in achievement level they are still very low.

Communication is certainly important, but more seems to be needed than communication. The last chapter attempts to sketch a proposal that would put things in their proper psychological priority for the deaf child: first, acceptance of the deaf person and his way of life; second, the thinking and feeling self; third, communication; fourth, language (English); and fifth, speech. With the priorities in this order we again consider the profoundly deaf child during his early years at home, the growing child at school, and the deaf adult in his society.

9 The Order of Priorities

This chapter is a short summary and an outlook. No new data will be discussed; rather, three crucial priorities pertaining to the deaf child's healthy development and learning will be singled out. Our aim is to construct a perspective on deafness that would break with the past by putting language where it belongs psychologically—not at the top or at the beginning, but four or five steps down.

The top priorities would be acceptance of deafness, of the deaf person, and of the community formed by deaf persons. Acceptance on the part of parents means recognizing the difference and taking it into account in a loving, intelligent manner. This first step is slow and painful for parents, and it is contrary to what parents unfortunately often hear: "Just treat the child like any other child." It is easy to seduce the parents of a deaf child with the expectation that their child will be "just like a hearing child." Normal parents are bound to fall for this message because it promises them what they wish to hear, but it makes unconditional acceptance even harder. It tells the child: "I love you—on the condition that you behave as if you were not deaf." That is, the condition stresses the weakest point in the deaf child's aptitude, his speech and his language. This form of denial is bound to place the child at an insurmountable disadvantage, and specialists with whom the parents come into contact should do everything they can to make acceptance as painless, as rapid, and as total as possible.

Early, reliable diagnosis of auditory status is a basic requisite, and it must be followed by a realistic appraisal of whether the child is hard of hearing and belongs in the hearing world or whether he is deaf and will need to become a member of the deaf community. Parents must be informed realistically about the potential help of hearing aids. They need the solid foundation of reality on which to plan the future of their child, not the false hope that their deaf child is going to be the one exception in a hundred or a thousand who will make it in the hearing world without the deaf community. No child or parent should be given the burden to prove himself as extraordinary. Let us sensibly look after the average person; the exceptional person will find his own way, because almost by definition he cannot be put into a general framework.

Acceptance of the deaf community, not as a world apart from the hearing world but as a different world within our world, is priority number one for the society at large. If society really wants to help deaf people, to upgrade their economic opportunities, and to improve their quality of life, they should do this in consultation and cooperation with responsible deaf adults and their associations, rather than pretending that "we know what is best for them." To propose to deaf people that ideally their lives should be similar to that of hearing persons so that no deaf community would be needed is a second form of denial which undermines the necessary basis of mutual respect and understanding.

Acceptance of the thinking and feeling deaf child who is growing into an adult is priority number one for education. These three forms of acceptance of deafness—at home, at school, and in society—would effectively reverse our perspective on deafness and would break the historical link of speechlessness and stupidity. Deaf persons—young and old, with or without speech, with much or little knowledge of the English language, successful or unsuccessful in academic programs—could then be treated as intelligent persons according to their stage of development and could be given the opportunity to use their personal resources in the most constructive and socially useful manner.

As the deaf child grows up and enters classes and schools for deaf children, some basic changes can be proposed which go beyond methods to the underlying philosophy of education. In short, education should continue to make real the psychological acceptance and encouragement of what is good and strong in the deaf child. As indicated in previous chapters, what we need is not merely an innovative and more adequate method for doing the same thing; we need to ask whether the goals are appropriate. Educators quarrel about the method but seem to agree on the ultimate goal: to make the education of deaf children as nearly as possible a replica of the education of hearing children, which is clearly a form of denial of deafness that cannot be missed by the deaf child.

Recall for a moment some of the findings of chapters 5 and 6. We observed that the intellectual development of deaf children in many instances resembles the development of children from culturally and socially impoverished areas. We used the term *experiential deficiency* to describe the intellectual poverty in which deaf children grow up. How do the hearing children from impoverished areas fare at school? What does education do for them? Does it help them break out of the circle of poverty? Does it provide occasions of success? Does it strengthen their feeling of self-value? No; rather, it puts language and reading as the indispensable precondition that will make all other desirable goals come true. How tragic for these hearing children and what poor psychology! And how similar their plight is to the condition of deaf children.

Is it possible that the educators of deaf children could take the bold step of breaking with the unhealthy educational tradition that has almost completely forgotten the thinking of the growing child and put language and reading as the immediate primary goal of early education? Educators of deaf children have every reason to do so. Their clients are so poor in language that to wait for them to become good readers before nourishing their intellectual development is an almost sure way to deny them intellectual food entirely. On the other hand, both theory and research indicate that intelligence does not build on language, but rather, language builds on intelligence. Hence, if our educational aim is to produce adolescents who are motivated and able to read written material that can challenge their thinking, our first concern should be with the source of the intelligent use of language and not with the medium of language as such. A "school for thinking" rather than a school for language or reading would be important for all young children, bright or dull, poor or rich, but for none is it more urgent than for deaf children.

This is not the place to repeat what has been said about the intellectual and personality aspects of the child's development. Development springs from inner sources in the person and is nothing but the child's developing intelligence. This intelligence is available to the deaf child in plenty; it makes use of symbols or produces them as necessary. Verbal language is the last and most difficult medium, which is suitable for the adult intelligence, but it is by no means the chief medium or occasion for earlier development.

Is education ready for radical changes? Change does not come easily, especially in the institutionalized setting of education. On the other hand, some remarkable innovations are taking place in education in general. Changes that nobody would have predicted some years ago are now occurring in the education of the deaf child, and this may be merely a hint of what could and should happen in all education.

Significantly, educators of deaf children are realizing that sympathetic understanding of deaf people must be the basis for the education of deaf children (Scherer 1971). Traditionally the formal training of teachers of deaf children or of speech therapists has not provided this long-range perspective. You recall that this book started with a description of the deaf community to help you see who deaf people are and how they live. Just as instruction methods for deaf youngsters are of limited use unless the teacher understands the deaf community, so also compilations of researched data on deaf persons do not make much sense without this understanding.

If the main ideas of the psychology of the deaf person as presented in earlier chapters are applied to the formation of the new goal in education, we would have a school for thinking in which the psychological priorities of the growing deaf child would be taken seriously. The school would encourage the initiative of the thinking and feeling self and would subordinate all activities to this primary goal. The school would not slavishly imitate traditional schools for hearing children or put all its emphasis on any one method of teaching language or speech. Thus the longstanding conflict over methods of teaching would recede in importance, as teachers would be directed to ask themselves the crucial question: Are the majority of school activities in which the deaf child engages appropriate and challenging to his present status? When teachers will be able to give an honest yes to this question, a new day for the education of the deaf child will have arrived. Here above all a sound psychology can make a profound, revolutionary contribution to the topic of deafness and learning.

Appendix 1:
A Thinking Laboratory for Deaf Children

The following is a modified version of a speech given at Milton, Ontario, School for the Deaf, May 19, 1970. It describes some practical applications for the ideas discussed in the text:

I would like to share a few observations from our center[1] that should help you in your difficult work as teachers of deaf children. Our research with deaf children and adults has led to a considerable amount of valuable new knowledge about psychology in general as well as about the psychology of deaf children. Moreover, much that can be used in the education of deaf children is just as suitable for hearing children. In fact, the education of hearing children often lacks many of the things which education for deaf children lacks; the difference is that deaf children are a much bigger educational problem, and for that reason we should be more motivated to try something new and constructive.

When you ask a teacher—either of deaf children or of hearing children—"Do you think that education and school in general should challenge the mind of the child?" there can be only one answer, "Of course it should, no question about it." I presented this question to a few elementary teachers of hearing children and then continued, "Well, tell me an activity in your class that challenges the child's mind." The teacher looks at me, hesitates, and hardly knows what to say. Then fortunately she thinks of numbers and says, "Well, we've worked with numbers." Apparently she thinks this should be challenging.

Much of our educational system is not designed to challenge the child's mind. There are many reasons—maybe unconsciously we do not want the schools to challenge the child's mind, we do not want mature citizens who think. But we live in troubled times, and traditional values are changing. Young people are dissatisfied with many aspects of social and political life (so are we), and they want to do something about it. As educators we face an awe-

---

[1] The thinking laboratory was under the supervision of Sydney Wolff. This program is continuing under Mr. Wolff's direction at the Department of Special Education, State University College, Geneseo, New York.

some challenge in helping these young persons, and although we may not have the right answer to every question, we can attempt to develop children who use their minds, not only in the narrow areas of logic and science but also in social and human relations, in creativity, in all of life. I am sure you share the same challenge; you want deaf children to grow up as thinking and feeling human beings. This is the theme I want to discuss: How can we as teachers help to bring up children who will be thinking human beings, who will constructively confront whatever problems they meet as they become adults? Many problems that seem peculiar to deaf children are really not so different from the problems of ordinary students.

I am talking here about the thinking human person, and in particular about the thinking child. First I should explain what I mean by a thinking mind. One does not have to be a psychologist to have some notions about "thinking"; all of us have some ideas about what thinking means, what knowledge means, and what intelligence means, quite apart from intelligence tests. I am proposing here that thinking, knowing, and intelligence, in a general sense, refer to the same thing. Within the framework in which I now speak, intelligence refers to the specific competence of the human person to behave intelligently; when we employ the word *thinking* we emphasize intelligent behavior, using knowledge intelligently, solving a problem according to intelligent norms.

The word *intelligence* is often understood in much too narrow a sense. We often suppose that intelligence and thinking belong to just a narrow part of physical and logical reality, apart from which exist perception, emotions, values, motivation, and other things—as if one could neatly partition life. Intelligence is not something added to behavior; rather, some level of intelligence is present in any kind of human behavior, otherwise it would not be human behavior at all. Consider then that thinking and intelligence are as broad as life is, and there is no area in human life to which intelligence cannot be applied. Obviously one cannot apply intelligence in the same way to moral and social areas as one can apply it to the physical sciences, but there is intelligence —an active human mind—behind all forms of human behavior, and one should not limit intelligence to just one area of life.

What I am proposing is a new theory of intelligence. Piaget is the only great psychologist who holds a theory of thinking that makes sense of the fact that deaf children can grow up into thinking human beings even though they do not know much language. In other words, all other theories of thinking assign language such a predominant role, they make language such a determining factor of the developing mind, that if the theories were true a deaf child could not grow up into a thinking human being. I refer to a deaf child who has not mastered the language of society. Surely you and I know many hundred deaf youngsters who know language very poorly, but who are nevertheless adequate, thinking, intelligent human beings. This is a very important fact that is available for everybody to see. If you do not see it, you simply do not want to see it. If a theory of intelligence is based on the fact that human language is a major determiner, it would be impossible for such "thinking without language" to exist.

When I ask a teacher, "Do you provide activities that challenge the child's thinking," an intelligent answer can only be given if the teacher knows what thinking is—and I would be surprised if in your training to become teachers much thought was given to this particular concept. We learn about individual differences and about IQ tests, but IQ tests simply tell you how children differ on a certain dimension, on a certain standardized performance. They do not clarify the basic factors of thinking and intelligence.

Because I had observed deaf children grow up into thinking human beings, I was forced to look for a theory that made sense of this fact, and Piaget's is such a theory. He concluded that thinking is not primarily based on language. According to Piaget, development of thinking—that is, the development of the thinking child—occurs through the child's activity within his physical and social environment, and language, far from being the preferred medium of development of the mind, is actually much too difficult a medium for a young mind. In other words, *it requires a developed intelligence to use language intelligently.* You can observe this for yourselves. For instance, many eight-year-old children have a reasonably accurate idea of the concept of probability—the likelihood that something will happen, like 50/50, 80/20, not at all, or definitely yes. I can show their knowledge of probability by playing nonverbal games with them. But the child cannot express this verbally, nor can he give you the definition of probability (I could hardly ask *you* to do this because it is quite difficult). Also, the child would not comprehend a purely verbal lecture on probability; it would just go in one ear and out the other. Language is therefore a difficult tool that is often unsuitable unless the mind is fully developed.

The concept of probability is just one example of what I mean by thinking and intelligence. When I use these words, and when Piaget talks about the theory of knowing, he refers to the broad framework within which thinking takes place; he does not single out particular instances but refers to the general human competence to behave intelligently. These broad concepts of classes, relations, numbers, probabilities, and so on are the framework within which all human thinking takes place whether the person goes to school or not, whether he lives now or lived five hundred years earlier, whether he lives here or in New Zealand. This is the essential human capacity for intellectual functioning. It is the basis on which any specific skill must rest if it is to be more than a rote skill. Language is a very difficult skill for thinking, so difficult that most adults have difficulty assimilating and understanding propositions. I propose the following relation between language and thinking, fully realizing that it is difficult to change a way of thinking that has been assumed and used for many years.

Language is a principal and preferred medium of thinking for a developed mind, for an adult mind, for a mind that has reached, as Piaget calls it, the formal operatory stage. There is no question about it: what I am writing could not have been done if I did not have a formalized language and a mind capable of expressing this kind of language and if your minds were not capable of reading and assimilating this language. You can deal with propositions and you can assimilate them, because you are capable of structural thinking to which you can assimilate the verbal propositions I am communicating. But children are not born with these structures. Children first manifest what

Piaget calls instinctive and sensorimotor schemes or structures; then comes a long period of preoperatory schemes. When a child is about six years old he begins to enter a period called the concrete operatory stage, which means that the child acquires his first stable ideas of classes, relations, probabilities, time, place, and so on, but he can deal with them properly only in context with concrete realities. When the child is about twelve or thirteen years old his mind develops to the formal operatory stage. At that point the mind can deal with verbal propositions such as the one I am offering.

Because language is such a tremendously important and useful tool for the developed mind, we fall into the wrong belief that language is the primary food for the developing mind. This is the fallacy I would like you to guard against. If we really want to provide opportunities for a child to develop his mind—and I think the school should be a place where we do this—we should realize that language per se is in many ways an inappropriate tool. The most telling example of this is the existence of deaf children who certainly develop their minds, at least up to the stage of concrete operatory thinking. Where deaf persons in general fall short is at the formal operatory level. More precisely, what happens is that they barely reach formal operatory thinking, and then they cannot develop their minds much further because they do not have the tool of language.

I do not mean to minimize the ultimate importance of language. But I do suggest to all teachers that the appropriate medium for helping the developing mind is not verbal language. For instance, if we want to help children to understand the concept of probability, we do not give them definitions of probability in verbal propositions; rather, we put the child in a concrete situation where he can observe probability events. Our experiments with both deaf and hearing children have demonstrated that deaf children reach the concrete operatory stage just about the same time as the average hearing child, a finding that is tremendously interesting if you think of its implication. Hearing children are completely surrounded by the linguistic environment from the earliest age, and they thus hear many verbal expressions of time relations, yet these hearing children must wait until they are six or seven years old before they develop their first real understanding of time as expressed in words like *day, week, month, year.* Simply being exposed to a word is therefore not enough. Now compare this situation with that of deaf children, who hardly ever use an expression that has to do with time. When they are seven years old, they too understand time concepts. These observations (and many others of this type) show that the basic development of intellectual competence is largely independent of the linguistic environment. The deaf child learns concepts of time, classifying, relations, and numbers as well as a hearing child. We should remember this, and it should help us to treat deaf children as the intelligent human beings they are. (This is equally true of hearing children who may have difficulty with reading, writing, or language skills.)

To illustrate how we are testing probability thinking, imagine the following situation. You have a small bag and marbles of two colors—say, twenty yellow and twenty blue marbles. The child is told to put ten yellow marbles and two blue marbles into the bag. Then you shake the bag and let the child pick out a marble; but before he does this you say, "Stop, what color do you think this marble will be?"—you know from working with deaf children that it is not difficult to indicate to them what you want. Instead of a verbal response, they can point to the color (if these instructions are still too difficult, one starts with a simpler game). So the children know that the bag contains ten yellow marbles and two blue marbles. Try this once with six-year-old children. Give the children another set of ten yellow marbles and two blue marbles so that they have in front of them an exact replica of the marbles that are in the bag; it is therefore not a question of memory. When you now ask a child, "What color do you think will come out?" many six-year-old children will say, "Yellow." Indeed, if the child is lucky, it will be a yellow marble. Of course it could be a blue marble, in which case the young child would exclaim, "I was wrong," when actually his guess was correct. Most six-year-old children, deaf or hearing, after they take out a yellow marble and you continue asking for guesses will say, "Blue," according to alternating chances. In other words, most six-year-old children have a poor concept of probability. They know it is not sure either one way or the other, but they do not really understand the proportion, and having nine yellow and two blue marbles in front of them is of little help. Let the children observe that sometimes even if there is only one blue marble versus twenty yellow marbles, one can still draw out a blue marble the first time. This kind of concrete probability situation helps the child develop his mind. Whether the child uses words in this game is largely irrelevant. We could not even teach the child these things if we only used words and did not have the concrete event in front of him. What is true of probability is true of all the other concepts I have mentioned, such as classifying objects, putting them in order or in correspondence, or understanding relations of space, perspective, and physical transformation.

These concepts, which Piaget has studied, provide the general framework within which thinking takes place. The school, whether for hearing children or for deaf children, should make a conscious effort to provide thinking experiences for children to show off their developing minds. I am using the words *show off* purposely. I would hate to say "teach intelligence" or "teach thinking" because we cannot teach these things; all we can do is provide the opportunity, because the source of development of the thinking mind is within the child. The child must be active, must operate on the environment. Many people misunderstand this to mean that the environment is unnecessary, that one could simply keep a child alive and after twelve years would find that he is a normal operatory child. This is nonsense of course, because the environment is not something added to the organism; the organism and environment are two sides of the same coin, parts of a larger evolutionary history. Obviously the environment can be more or less conducive to development; it provides food and opportunities. You cannot have a healthy plant if you do not feed it properly, and if the plant is basically sick, even the best food is not going to make it get well. That is how we should think about developing the human child.

The human child carries within him the wherewithal to grow and develop, and you do not have to give him candy to motivate him. Every child wants to develop. Every child has this motivation. As a simple proof of this, take any five-year-old child and look at him two years later. He is going to be more intelligent than he was two years earlier, and that would not happen if he were not motivated to grow intellectually. The reason teachers often worry so much about motivation is because they deal with activities which in themselves are not conducive to the developing mind, activities such as reading, writing, and language skills. For a six- to 10-year-old child these are quite secondary things, and I would like to assign them the secondary emphasis they deserve. Unless we develop the healthy mind of a child, teaching language is not going to be of much help. We want to develop children who can use language intelligently, and the primacy here is on the intelligent mind.

We should introduce thinking activities into the classroom, particularly for the elementary school child, not as luxuries or as frills but as primary activities which would give the child the following message: "I like you the way you are. I like you as a human being. I want you to show off your thinking. I want you to show me how clever you are. I want you to enjoy yourself in your thinking activity and to try out your thinking in a wide area of activities, whether it has to do with visual thinking, motor behavior, drama, the arts, or social, moral, logical, and physical thinking." Only when this primary message is firmly established in the child and the child goes along with us would I put pressure on language achievement as such. With thinking as the primary emphasis the child will be on your side. If a child is intellectually alive and active, he will spontaneously search for ways of symbolizing and communicating.

Every young child enjoys playing the kind of thinking games we are talking about, even though some of these thinking games are highly abstract, like symbol logic. We hardly believed it ourselves when we discovered that seven-year-old deaf children were fascinated by symbol logic, as were children from Indian reservations and black children from the inner city. Fifteen-year-olds may get bored by it and say it is not relevant because they have gone through a period of frustration, and they present quite a different problem. Unfortunately, the school provides thinking activities for students all too rarely; when the school does offer thinking games it is mainly because an imaginative teacher is intuitively doing the right thing. Exciting things are being done in many schools for deaf children, but it is frequently despite the school structure rather than within the school structure.

Many teachers ask how they could make their school "a school for thinking." In my book "Piaget for Teachers"[2] I describe a series of suitable activities; some of them we have tried ourselves, some of them I observed in other places. It is easy to fill a whole school day with meaningful activities that are primarily geared to thinking activities. By all means let us include language and reading as a secondary goal if the child is ready, but let our primary concern not be with the activities but with the underlying philosophy. It is psychologically unsound to force a child into a curriculum when he is not ready and when he is not motivated. Most of what we teach in a hearing elementary school are

---

[2] H. G. Furth, *Piaget for teachers*. Englewood Cliffs, N. J.: Prentice-Hall, 1971. The activities of a school for thinking are described in greater detail in H. G. Furth and H. Wochs, *Thinking goes to school: Piaget's theory in practice*. Champaign, Ill.: Research Press, 1973. In press.

relatively simple skills, like reading and numbers. Many of us acquire some part of these skills even before going to school, and that is the normal way to learn these things. To consider these as primary activities and to judge both the elementary teacher and the pupil at this age level by such criteria is telling the child that he is not here primarily to think but to do the skills that the adults of the society have deemed necessary.

In a small demonstration project in the West Virginia State School for the Deaf we introduced a laboratory for thinking to which the children came one period every day. The project continued for one and a half years. The purpose of this lab was to give the children an opportunity to show off their intellectual skills without being handicapped by their inadequate knowledge of language. We focused on tasks that could be given without verbal instructions. Most deaf children, as you well know, can catch on to the instructions, particularly when they have concrete material. So we played games like the probability game and games of classifying or visual thinking. We continued these games over several days, dropped them for some weeks, and then brought them back later. Some of these games involved all eight children in the class; others could be played by two or three children. The children themselves were active; sometimes two or three would ask the teacher, "Can I play this game with another child?" You will agree that this was an ideal learning situation; every teacher wishes that his pupils would work independently so that the teacher then has time to help other children.

For visual thinking games we displayed figures on the blackboard, and the children had to imagine and draw what the figures would look like when they were turned around, up, or down or to the left or right. These are quite difficult tasks for six- to eight-year old children, hearing or deaf; these tasks challenge the operatory structures the children are beginning to develop. For perspective games we would show an assembly of objects on a table and ask, "What does the assembly look like from various angles?" In all these activities the children were not given verbal instructions; rather, they were given the opportunity to try things out and to observe for themselves what things look like. If a child insisted on an explanation, we would try to encourage another child to explain to this child, rather than provide the answer ourselves.

For symbol logic games we used logical symbols, some of which you can find in a logic book, like conjunction, disjunction, and negation, but we illustrated them with pictures. The children had to use their intelligence to understand the matching of logical sentences and pictures. For instance, we would use the letter H for house and the letter B for blue. We would then present the logical expression "not house and blue." That is, we symbolized the combination of something that is not a house and at the same time is blue. Then would come an arrow which would indicate "is an instance of," and the child's task would be to draw a picture that would satisfy this requirement. "Not house and blue" can be verified by many different things; it is not just a question of one question and one answer, it is understanding what this formula means. A child might choose to draw a blue tree or a blue pencil. Subsequently the task would be indicated by means of a crossed arrow that indicated "is *not* an instance of"—that is, you ask for wrong instances. How often do teachers ask a pupil to give wrong answers? But certainly intelligence is not exhausted by learning one answer to a certain question. Intelligence is at all times a constructing by the individual, one of many ways of looking at things. In all these activities that I have described, the point is not so much having one question and one right answer as applying a generalized structure to potentially varying situations.

This demonstration lab worked very well. The deaf children benefited from it in thinking and particularly in personal and social behavior. We had proposed that children who had a fixed period of school activity for thinking would be in a better position to learn and to use language for the rest of the day than children who were not given this opportunity. A control group was given special language activities during the same time that the experimental group participated in thinking activities. The results showed that the children who went to the thinking lab grew in thinking skills a little more than the control children, and linguistically they were in no way behind the control children. This is some indication that taking time out of the school day for thinking is not going to harm children.

Obviously these results are not striking enough to convince the skeptic about the usefulness of this program. But then, this was not a full program where, instead of just for twenty minutes a day, the whole school day and the entire year would be permeated by thinking activities. If deaf children were exposed to such a program for a number of years, they might surprise us, just as those seven-year-old deaf youngsters surprised us with their manipulation of logical symbols.

Perhaps you are impressed with the possibilities of intellectual achievements in deaf children but are still unhappy because I have not mentioned language and speech. Can you understand why deaf children could succeed on logical and mathematical tasks that would challenge you and me but could fail to comprehend a sentence that any four-year-old finds easy? The answer in a nutshell is that logic is necessary but language is arbitrary. Logic is necessary in more than one sense—it is logically necessary and it is psychologically necessary. If we as teachers realize these psychological priorities and help deaf children to feel more like thinking human beings, we have every reason to expect that they will have more to talk about and will be better motivated in the formal learning of the arbitrary and therefore difficult skill of verbal language.

Appendix 2:
Overview of Educational Opportunities for the Profoundly Deaf Child in the United States, by Sydney Wolff

Since education in the United States is primarily the concern of the states and of local districts, it is to be expected that education for deaf children across the country differs in the availability and variety of specific educational programs. Nevertheless there is sufficient commonality in the general approach to the education of deaf children so that most of the educational opportunities listed below are available in most states.

The first step in the education of a deaf child is the education of the child's parents. Most deaf children are born to hearing parents who have no knowledge of deafness. Most of them are first diagnosed as deaf by family doctors, pediatricians, or eye-ear-nose and throat specialists whose understanding of deafness is focused on deafness as a sensory deprivation. Many parents are given the unrealistic hope that hearing aids and traditional speech therapy will overcome the deficits of profound hearing loss. Only rarely do parents see a teacher of the deaf, or another deaf person, or anyone with an understanding of the social and educational implications of deafness, until the children reach school age. Many parents try alone to learn to live with the grief and the guilt they feel for their deaf child.

It is an unfortunate fact that the advice which is most frequently given to parents of a young deaf child is both inadequate and misleading. For many parents the search for an adequate diagnosis is in itself a traumatic experience. The parents have frequently fought through a series of opinions ranging from mental retardation to emotional disturbance. They have had to accept or reject suggestions of their own incompetence, over-protectiveness, neurotic concern. The true diagnosis of deafness frequently comes as a relief.

When deafness is understood only as a physical dysfunction, then the essential differentness of the deaf child is seen as the inability to speak. The doctor who recommends a speech clinic, and the speech therapist who teaches speech to the child are seeing the deaf child through the biases of their own perspectives. The parents are only too happy to go along with this advice

This is the first publication of this essay. Permission to reprint must be obtained from the author and publisher.

because, above all, they want a normal child. The deaf child is being trained to live in a hearing world; that is, he is being trained to be normal. The parents' deep emotional need to believe in the ultimate success of this under-taking prolongs their guilt and sorrow, and delays their acceptance of the child as he really is.

Unfortunately, a deep seated conflict about the manner of teaching lan-guage to deaf children has preoccupied deaf educators for more than a cen-tury. This oral-manual controversy over methods has interfered with a free and constructive discussion of general educational issues and penalized par-ents who want to make responsible decisions. Whatever the ideological merits of a theory or personal inclinations of a parent, the overriding fact is that, no matter how early speech training begins, nor how expertly it is done, the pre-lingual deaf child has little chance to acquire genuinely usable speech. Very few deaf adults would attempt to transact any business, such as buying a plane ticket, without a pad and a pencil with which to communicate.

Thus, the early, vital, language-forming years in a deaf child's life are too often wasted in the attempt to make the child "normal." And when the parents have finally come to accept the truth of deafness, the child is thirteen or four-teen with little language, and less speech.

Every parent of a deaf child needs a deaf adult as a friend. Every large community has a deaf population, and many have clubs for the deaf. Parents can go to the deaf community to ask for help. They will be warmly received and generously aided. No one with a deaf friend will long view deafness as an insurmountable handicap, or as a grievous abnormality. Further, the parent will have an experienced advisor to help him learn about his own child. A realistic understanding of deafness is the only thing that can help the parent overcome his shock and grief. Deaf children of deaf parents generally do not have the difficulties in school that deaf children of hearing parents have. Deaf parents naturally provide a manual communication system for their deaf or hearing children. And they can accept and respect their children without the guilt that hearing parents feel.

The deaf child's future is immensely improved if his parents have a healthy and realistic attitude toward deafness. With the real acceptance of the child's loss, the parents will inevitably learn to communicate with the child, instead of insisting that the child learn to communicate with them. With com-munication, the parents will learn that deaf children are in no substantial way inferior to hearing children, and from their respect for him, the child will learn a healthy respect for himself.

Counseling services to help parents reach a full acceptance of the deaf child as outlined above are only available to a very few families, generally in metropolitan areas. Most states simply have no organization to support this service. The Bureau of the Physically Handicapped of the state's Department of Education will have information on counseling services in specific com-munities. Even where counseling is available, it is very helpful for parents to meet other hearing parents of deaf children. To this end there are now na-tional and local organizations which parents can join. Sharing information and experiences will reduce the parents' feelings of isolation.

The school for the deaf will probably be the most helpful and supportive institution within the state. Whether or not parents plan to send their child to the school, the school will provide answers to questions, both general and specific, about all aspects of deafness. They will also provide names and addresses of local parent groups, associations of the deaf, and of parents and deaf people in specific communities.

Early Childhood Programs
(Ages 1 to 4)

A growing number of schools, both public and private, have early childhood programs, which begin before the child is old enough to attend regular classes. The most common beginning of educational instructions for deaf children are weekly or daily speech lessons available in *speech and hearing clinics*. Clinics serving metropolitan areas sometimes also offer educational classes for children. Parents who live in smaller communities may be limited by transportation problems. Many parents who visit schools for the deaf are invited to participate in *institutes* for parents of preschool deaf children. Usually the parents and the children stay at the school for a few days, and attend lectures, films, training sessions, and discussions on many aspects of deafness. For many parents these institutes can be a first reassuring experience concerning the problems of deafness.

If the family is fortunate enough to live in an area in which an early childhood program is available, it will be one of two kinds of programs, home visitation or demonstration home. In *home visitation programs* the school sends a social worker or teacher to the home to instruct the parents in specific techniques to encourage the use of residual hearing and to help the child develop speech reading skills. In *demonstration home programs* the school provides a simulated home atmosphere at the school to accomplish the same ends. Most early childhood programs strictly follow the traditional oral approach. The John Tracy Clinic in Los Angeles is known for providing a free correspondence program with sequential lessons to encourage natural speech reading development. In addition, staff personally answer parent queries. The clinic focuses on the expectation of usable speech and speech reading and strongly discourages manual language. Apart from this one-sided emphasis many parents find long distance communication with an advisor frustrating and slow.

However a growing number of agencies can be found following the total approach that uses all means of communication, including manual language. Many other schools are now considering the adoption of this method in their preschool programs, even when they do not use it in earlier home training. Ideally the deaf child should have three things: a manual communication system together with maximum use of residual hearing at home, training in speech and speech reading at a clinic, and the opportunity to participate in an early childhood education program.

For some parents a preschool program represents an opportunity to turn the burden of responsibility for the child's education over to the school. While it is true that the school is organized to accept such responsibility, parents should realize the limitation of an early intervention that is not fully seconded by the home. After a few years in school, children who have been in preschool programs do not often show significant differences in speech, speech reading, and academic achievement, compared to non-preschool children. A significant benefit to the child, not always measurable, is the contact with other deaf children with whom he can share experiences as an equal.

Regular School Programs
(Ages 3 to 19)

There are a multitude of regular school programs available to deaf children in the United States. Each state supports one or several *public residential schools,* some of which require students to spend weekends at home. Many communities offer *public day schools* or day classes. In some areas public classes for the multihandicapped deaf are also available. For special cases parents may seek schools that have special programs, but generally schools for the deaf provide for these children.

There are also many *private residential* and *day schools* in the country. Some of these are partially supported by public funds. Services range widely in price. Those schools that can select their pupils usually follow traditional oral approaches, but a few offer specialized or innovative programs.

A very few communities offer day classes that *integrate* hearing and deaf children. The James Madison School in the Santa Ana, California, school district has experimented with integrating hearing children into classes for the deaf, and teaching the hearing children total communication skills. The children also participate in extracurricular activities with the deaf children. The school has also involved the parents in its activities.

Methodologies

Within the framework of regular school programs several methods of instruction are utilized. The *oral* method, which for over a century has been forcefully advocated by the A. G. Bell Society, relies on speech and speech reading. Schools, particularly private schools, which use this method insist generally on the exclusive use of it, in the dormitories as well as in the classrooms.

Some schools supplement oral communication with *fingerspelling,* also called visible English or the Rochester method. In these situations the teachers and students speak and fingerspell simultaneously. These schools insist upon the correct transmission of the structure of English, and the teachers always spell total sentences.

A third method, which is today supported by the National Association of the Deaf, is called *total communication.* In this system all methods of communication are used and encouraged because all can contribute to the acquisition of a usable language system by the deaf child. In the past schools have used the oral system until the child is perhaps twelve and then begun total communication in the middle and advanced schools. Some schools now, however, begin total communication when the child first enters school at age three or four. It is probably safe to assume that many public schools which have used only the oral method in the early years, will now introduce total communication from the start.

In all these methodologies communication in the classroom is supplemented by written instructions and by a battery of sophisticated teaching aids. Classrooms for the deaf generally have loop hearing aids that amplify the teacher's voice into individual portable hearing aids adjusted to individual student needs.

Types of Programs

Regular school programs for the deaf student generally cover the child's education between ages three or four to eighteen or nineteen. The program is usually divided into three parts: the primary school which children leave at eleven or twelve, the middle school for children to fifteen, and the upper or advanced school which in unusual circumstances can keep students until they are twenty-one.

Apart from using special approaches to teach speech, speech reading and language, programs in schools for the deaf follow those of traditional education for hearing children. However, grade level does not closely reflect academic achievement; breadth and depth of subject matter is usually limited and the pace is slower and involves much more repetition than in hearing schools. What is special, then, is the environment and not so much the education.

Speech and language development are stressed at all levels, but there is an increasing emphasis on subject matter and prevocational training in the middle and advanced departments. By the second year of the middle school the child is usually in one of three tracks, academic, general, or vocational. Some schools have state-accredited high schools for those going on to college.

Many schools offer vocational programs in such areas as printing, auto repair, computer operations, woodworking, beauty culture, shoe repair, horticulture, tailoring, baking, and secretarial skills. Although vocational programs have steadily grown so that many schools have erected new vocational buildings, some schools have developed a cooperative arrangement with industries and with other schools in the community in order to offer a variety of work-study programs.

Post-Secondary Education

A variety of post-secondary opportunities are available to young deaf adults after completion of the high school program. Gallaudet College in

Washington, D. C., offers a liberal arts education and a master's program in education for those planning to teach the deaf. The National Technical Institute for the Deaf (attached to the Rochester Institute of Technology) in Rochester, New York, provides technical and vocational programs in an integrated setting. There are other technical and vocational schools and colleges that have developed programs to integrate deaf students. For a current listing of programs available see *The American Annals of the Deaf, Directory of Programs and Services.*

A very few deaf students have also succeeded in colleges with no special programs for the deaf. But probably a more efficient integration of deaf subjects into hearing college populations can be accomplished in those colleges that offer supplemental programs for the deaf.

For those students who do not go to college and yet need further vocational training, state vocational rehabilitation services are available. They provide further job training, often coupled with counseling and job placement services. There is also a recent growing interest in adult education leading to increased vocational opportunities for the deaf person.

Conclusion

It is a sad fact that even after many years most parents cannot communicate with their deaf children. As deaf children grow to maturity they will turn to their deaf peers for meaningful communication. Parents who can fully communicate with their children, regardless of method, will naturally provide a most significant part of those children's education.

Parents are unfortunately exposed to a confusing lack of agreement regarding educational policies. Although far from perfect, the climate today is more conducive than it has been before to a realistic evaluation and responsible decision-making on the part of parents of deaf children.

Nationally too, horizons for deaf people are growing: news programs on national television are simultaneously being interpreted in Sign language, the National Theatre of the Deaf travels and performs all over the world, Sesame Street has added a deaf actor to its company of players, more and more hearing people attend classes in Sign language, a deaf man does a television commercial in Sign language while it is interpreted in speech for hearing people. With a growing understanding of deaf persons will come more opportunities. The stigma of deafness is on the wane: deaf people are people who are only deaf.

Sources of Information

The following publications are an effective way to gain insight into various aspects of deafness and into current educational trends and research.

The Deaf American
814 Thayer Avenue
Silver Spring, Maryland 20910
(Publication of the National Association of the Deaf)

American Annals of the Deaf
5034 Wisconsin Avenue, N. W.
Washington, D. C. 20016
(Publication of the Convention of American Instructors of the Deaf)

For information on the Parent Section write to:

Mrs. Lee Katz, President, Parent Section CAID
11210 Healy Street
Silver Spring, Maryland 20902

The Volta Review
1537 35th Street, N. W.
Washington, D. C. 20007
(Publication of Alexander Graham Bell Association for the Deaf. Also
has an International Parents Organization)

Appendix 3:
Behavior Inventory

Behavior Inventory

Rater Background

Name _____   Age _____

Sex _____   Occupation _____

Education _____   Rating Date _____

How long have you known the person rated? _____

Rated Person's Background

Name _____   Age _____

Sex _____   Occupation _____

Highest Grade Achieved _____   Marital Status _____

Directions

Read each statement carefully and consider whether the individual rated behaves in the manner described. Rate each item simply as True (T) or Not True (N) by checking the appropriate column. In this connection True (T) means that the item is "more true" or "more typical" than its opposite and also that it is on balance "more true than false." Similarly, Not True means that the item is "more false" or "less typical" than its opposite and also that it is on balance "more false than true."

Base your rating primarily on observed behavior and your own reactions to the individual; avoid second-hand information and psychological inferences. Make no effort to present a consistent portrait. Rate quickly; if you cannot decide, skip some items but come back to them at the end. Be sure to judge every item; if uncertain record your best guess.

		T	N
CC 1.	Rarely takes advantage of others for his own ends.	___	___
DA 2.	Doesn't ask for help even when in a jam.	___	___
ES 3.	Recovers quickly when he gets upset.	___	___
FY 4.	Tends to agree with someone in authority.	___	___
AA 5.	Tries to be friendly even when treated unfairly.	___	___
NW 6.	Rarely gives a hand to someone who needs help.	___	___
LD 7.	Tends to dominate conversations.	___	___
SD 8.	Engages in solitary recreation and amusement.	___	___
TT 9.	Confides his personal problems to others.	___	___
CO10.	Breaks promises when it seems useful to him.	___	___
DS11.	Tries to get opinions from others in making decisions.	___	___
EU12.	Often appears blue and down in the dumps.	___	___
FF13.	Says what he believes no matter who is around.	___	___
AH14.	Ridicules or belittles others.	___	___
NG15.	Gives help to peers who are having difficulty.	___	___
LP16.	Lets others take charge even though the responsibility is his.	___	___
SA17.	Acts close and personal with people.	___	___
TM18.	Says people don't understand him.	___	___
CC19.	Would feel badly if he had to lie to somebody.	___	___
DA20.	Will not ask for help in his school work even if he needs it.	___	___
ES21.	Appears cheerful under most circumstances.	___	___
FY22.	In discussions goes along with the will of the group.	___	___
AA23.	Is patient and tolerant of others' mistakes.	___	___
NW24.	Almost never gives a gift to anyone.	___	___
LD25.	Takes charge of things when he's with people.	___	___
SD26.	Avoids participating in group efforts.	___	___
TT27.	Acts trusting toward teachers and supervisors.	___	___
CO28.	Shows little or no gratitude for favors received.	___	___
DS29.	Is quick to turn to authority for solving his problems.	___	___
EU30.	Often appears listless and tired.	___	___
FF31.	Rarely pushed around by any of his friends.	___	___
AH32.	Makes unfavorable or hostile remarks about his peers.	___	___
NG33.	His friends tend to go to him when in trouble or feeling low.	___	___
LP34.	Dislikes taking on jobs calling for selling or persuasion.	___	___
SA35.	Tries to be included in most of his friends' activities.	___	___
TM36.	Says people criticize or blame him unjustly.	___	___
CC37.	Can distinguish between trivial offenses and serious wrong-doing.	___	___
DA38.	Keeps his troubles to himself.	___	___
ES39.	Can forget unpleasant events.	___	___
FY40.	Readily yields a point in an argument or discussion.	___	___
AA41.	Accepts teasing without undue irritation.	___	___
NW42.	Usually has an excuse to avoid lending his belongings to anyone.	___	___

T   N

LD43.   Bosses his friends and associates around.
SD44.   Stays away from social affairs where he might
        meet new people.   ___ ___
TT45.   Rarely complains of being misunderstood by others. ___ ___
CO46.   Tells lies if he can gain something by it.   ___ ___
DS47.   Is quick to ask for help on jobs he has taken on.   ___ ___
EU48.   Easily upset by his peers.   ___ ___
FF49.   Follows his own plan of action even when it is
        opposed by the group.   ___ ___
AH50.   Defiant and hostile toward persons in authority.   ___ ___

NG51.   Manifests a genuine interest in the problems
        of others.   ___ ___
LP52.   Enjoys being a follower rather than a leader.   ___ ___
SA53.   Expresses affection openly and directly through
        words and gestures.   ___ ___
TM54.   Misinterprets minor comments by others as
        unfavorable towards him.   ___ ___
CC55.   Can be depended upon to keep a promise.   ___ ___
DA56.   Rarely asks anyone for a favor.   ___ ___
ES57.   Can control his temper.   ___ ___
FY58.   Does what his more bossy peers ask him to do.   ___ ___
AA59.   Ignores his peers when they act nasty.   ___ ___
NW60.   Seems unable to act sympathetically when his
        peers are in trouble.   ___ ___

LD61.   Likes to volunteer advice when people have
        decisions to make.   ___ ___
SD62.   Rarely discusses his personal affairs.   ___ ___
TT63.   Is willing to disclose his personal affairs
        when asked.   ___ ___
CO64.   Gets around the rules or the law when it is
        useful to him.   ___ ___
DS65.   Goes to others for help and reassurance when
        in difficulty.   ___ ___

EU66.   Seems to be worried about some matter much of
        the time.   ___ ___
FF67.   Defends his viewpoint even when someone in
        authority disagrees.   ___ ___
AH68.   Readily shows anger or irritability in his
        dealings with others.   ___ ___
NG69.   Puts aside his own work or pleasure if somebody
        asks for help.   ___ ___
LP70.   Does not take initiative in suggesting new ways
        of doing things.   ___ ___

SA71.   Takes the initiative in making new acquaintances. ___ ___
TM72.   Complains of others prying into his affairs.   ___ ___
CC73.   Shows guilt when he has hurt a person's feelings.   ___ ___
DA74.   Avoids going to others for advice or sympathy.   ___ ___
ES75.   Seems to remain cool even in a crisis.   ___ ___

FY76.   Peers can easily change his opinion even if his
        mind was made up.   ___ ___
AA77.   When criticized justly, is ready to admit he's
        been at fault.   ___ ___
NW78.   Seldom cooperates or helps out in a chore even
        when asked.   ___ ___
LD79.   Talks his friends into doing what he would like.   ___ ___
SD80.   Keeps aloof from his peers.   ___ ___

TT81.   In general, thinks and speaks well of others.   ___ ___
CO82.   Takes advantage of his more gullible friends.   ___ ___

		T	N
DS83.	Seeks out people who show sympathy and concern for him.	___	___
EU84.	Some little thing gone wrong can spoil his whole day.	___	___
FF85.	His opinions are not easily changed by those around him.	___	___
AH86.	Tells people "off" when they annoy him.	___	___
NG87.	Lends things he values to his friends.	___	___
LP88.	Avoids positions of responsibility.	___	___
SA89.	Helps organize parties, dances, and celebrations.	___	___
TM90.	Slow to confide in others.	___	___

References

Furfey, P. H., and Harte, T. J. *Interaction of deaf and hearing in Baltimore City, Maryland.* Washington, D. C.: Catholic University of America Press, 1968.

Furth, H. G. Influence of language on the development of concept formation in deaf children. *Journal of Abnormal Social Psychology* 63 (1961): 386–89.

Furth, H. G. Research with the deaf: implications for language and cognition. *Psychological Bulletin* 3 (1964):145–64.

Furth, H. G. *Thinking without language: psychological implications of deafness.* New York: Free Press, 1966.

Furth, H. G. A comparison of reading test norms of deaf and hearing children. *American Annals of the Deaf* 111 (1966):461–62.

Furth, H. G. Linguistic deficiency and thinking: research with deaf subjects 1964–1969. *Psychological Bulletin* 76 (1971):58–72

Furth, H. G., and Youniss, J. The influence of language and experience on discovery and use of logical symbols. *British Journal of Psychology* 56 (1965):381–90.

Furth, H. G., and Youniss, J. Thinking in deaf adolescents: language and formal operations. *Journal of Communication Disorders* 2 (1969):195–202.

Furth, H. G., and Youniss, J. Formal operations and language: a comparison of deaf and hearing adolescents. *International Journal of Psychology* 6 (1971):49–64.

Gentile, A., and DiFrancesca, S. *Academic achievement test performance of hearing impaired students.* Washington, D. C.: Gallaudet College Press, 1969.

Lewis, M. M. *Language and Personality in deaf children.* Slough, Bucks.: National Foundation for Educational Research in England and Wales, 1963.

Meadow, K. P. Early manual communication in relation to the deaf child's intellectual, social, and communicative functioning. *American Annals of the Deaf* 113 (1968):29–41.

Oléron, P. *Recherches sur le developpement mental des sourds-muets.* Paris: Centre National de la Recherche Scientifique, 1957.

Oléron, P., and Herren, H. *L'acquisition des conservations et le langage: Etude comparative sur des enfants sourds et entendants.* Enfance 14 (1961): 203–219.

Quigley, S. P. The influence of fingerspelling on the development of language, communication, and educational achievement in deaf children. Urbana: Institute for Research on Exceptional Children, University of Illinois, 1969.

Rainer, J.; Altshuler, K.; Kallman, F.; and Deming, W., eds. *Family and mental health problems in a deaf population.* New York: Columbia University Press, 1963.

Robertson, A., and Youniss, J. Anticipatory visual imagery in deaf and hearing children. *Child Development* 40 (1969):123–35.

Ross, B. M. Probability concepts in deaf and hearing children. *Child Development* 37 (1966):653–62.

Schein, J. D. *The deaf community: Studies in the social psychology of deafness.* Washington, D. C.: Gallaudet College Press, 1968.

Scherer, P. A. An open letter to educators of the deaf. *American Annals of the Deaf* 116 (1971): 404–7.

Schlesinger, H. S., and Meadow, K. P. *Sound and Sign: Childhood Deafness and Mental Health.* Berkeley, Calif.: University of California Press, 1972.

Stuckless, E. R., and Birch, J. W. The influence of early manual communication on the linguistic development of deaf children. *American Annals of the Deaf* 111 (1966):452–60.

Vernon, McCay. Fifty years of research on the intelligence of deaf and hard of hearing children: A review of literature and discussion of implications. *Journal of Rehabilitation of the Deaf* 1 (1968):1–12.

Vernon, McCay, and Koh, Soon D. Effects of oral preschool compared to early manual communication on education and communication in deaf children. *American Annals of the Deaf* 116 (1971):569–74.

Index